Corporate Wonderland

Harri Hykkö

Corporate Wonderland

Thriving in the Corporate World While Staying True to You

The gendre fusion of poetry, surrealism and business literature

Design of cover: Harri Hykkö
Page layout: Harri Hykkö

Publisher: BoD · Books on Demand, Mannerheimintie 12 B,
00100 Helsinki, bod@bod.fi
Printing: Libri Plureos GmbH, Friedensallee 273,
22763 Hampuri, Saksa

ISBN: 978-952-80-9754-9

Twelve things that this book could do for readers:

1. Inspire Reflection: The book's poetic and introspective style can inspire readers to reflect on their own journey of self-discovery and personal growth.

2. Encourage Self-Exploration: Through its exploration of identity and self-realization, the book may motivate readers to embark on their own quests for personal understanding.

3. Foster Empowerment: The themes of resilience, hope, and self-acceptance can empower readers to face challenges and adversities with a positive mindset.

4. Promote Emotional Intelligence: By delving into the importance of acceptance and forgiveness in a corporate setting, the book may help readers develop emotional intelligence and navigate complex relationships.

5. Spark Creativity: The surreal and poetic language used in the book can ignite readers' creativity and encourage them to think outside the box.

6. Raise Awareness of Human Connection: The book's exploration of love and genuine human connections can heighten readers' awareness of the significance of relationships in our lives.

7. Enhance Understanding of the Corporate World: Readers may gain insights into the corporate world, including its jargon and complexities, which could be valuable for those navigating similar environments.

8. Offer Guidance for Personal Growth: Through the protagonist's journey, the book provides subtle guidance and lessons for personal growth and self-discovery.

9. Provide Perspective on the Corporate Environment: Readers working in corporate settings may gain a fresh perspective on the challenges and dynamics of the business world, particularly in relation to personal growth and relationships.

10. Offer Comfort and Relatability: The themes of self-acceptance, resilience, and the pursuit of authentic connections can provide comfort and relatability to readers facing similar challenges.

11. Encourage Open Conversations: The book's exploration of love and connection in a digital age may stimulate readers to engage in open discussions about the importance of genuine human interactions.

12. Celebrate the Power of Language: Through its use of poetic language and wordplay, the book showcases the beauty and expressive power of words, which may inspire readers to celebrate language and storytelling.

These aspects collectively make the book a rich source of inspiration, reflection, and guidance for its readers.

Chapter 1

The Odyssey of a Corporate Dreamer:
Lost in the Corporate Maze

The narrator's opening thoughts about being different 1

Amidst the corporate maze, I question my place,
Lost in the relentless chase, buzzwords and KPIs on my face.
With a holographic latte in hand, I ponder the scheme,
Am I just a cog in the wheel of the corporate dream?

In surreal PowerPoint visions, I feel out of sync,
As colleagues transform to spreadsheets, no time for a blink.
A unicorn in fluorescent hues trots on by,
Wearing a tie of bar graphs, aiming for the sky.

Am I the outlier, the disruptor they need?
In this sea of integration, where dreams must concede?
I yearn to pivot, to break the conformity's trance,
But words turn to data, I can't take the chance.

In the corridors of algorithms, I venture to explore,
This Wonderland of business, where dreams take flight and soar.
I seek to stand out in a landscape of metrics and schemes,
In this surreal realm of corporate dreams.

My footsteps echo in a chorus of data streams,
Each algorithmic beat a part of my grand schemes.
In this digital labyrinth, where numbers hold sway,
I aim to find my unique way.

Among the spreadsheets and charts, I find my ground,
Where data-driven decisions make a resounding sound.
But I aspire to be more than just a data point,
To leave an indelible mark on this corporate joint.

In the surreal realm of corporate dreams, I thrive,
Where innovation and ambition merge and strive.
I seek the elusive balance of profit and soul,
In this Wonderland of business, where stories unfold.

So I venture on, through the digital haze,
In pursuit of success in countless ways.
To stand out, to make a difference, it seems,
In the surreal realm of corporate dreams.

Chapter 2

The Quest for Digital Distinction

The narrator's opening thoughts about being different 2

In Biztopia's neon glow, where data reigns,
And profits climb, like endless chains,
I embark on a journey surreal,
Driven by corporate zeal.

Buildings transform, a PowerPoint parade,
Their windows pixels, metrics displayed.
I muse amidst this digital maze,
Of data-driven, profit-seeking days.

"A blockchain am I," my thoughts unfold,
"In this sea of tradition, my story's bold."
I ponder amidst suits with faces like codes,
Trading NFT handshakes in digital abodes.

A holographic skyscraper, ablaze with desire,
Spells "disruption" in flames, an innovation's fire.
In CRM software, the future seems bright,
In this surreal city of day and night.

In this realm, I seek to be unique,
An algorithmic anomaly, different yet sleek.
But thoughts morph swiftly, like bees in a hive,
Buzzing with efficiency, a digital drive.

I venture on, with courage untold,
Through landscapes of profit, of stories yet bold.
In this realm of surreal capitalism's reign,
I aim to disrupt, to break every chain.

I ventured forth, with courage in my heart,
Through landscapes of profit, from the very start.
In a world of surreal capitalism's embrace,
I aimed to bring change, to find my place.

Amidst boardrooms filled with suits and charts,
I sought to ignite new, ethical sparks.
Challenging norms, my mission was clear,
Within corporate landscapes, I had no fear.

With innovation as my trusty shield,
And purpose as my guide on this battlefield,
I embarked on a mission, hand in hand,
To redefine success in this corporate land.

In a world where capitalism's grip was tight,
I aimed to prove that doing right was right.
Breaking the chains of greed and exploitation's hold,
My pursuit was a future more equitable and bold.

Through challenges that lay ahead, I pressed on,
With a vision of a corporate world well-drawn.
In this surreal landscape, where ideals would reign,
I was determined to disrupt and break every chain.

I ventured forth, with courage untold,

Through landscapes of profit, stories yet bold.

In this realm of surreal capitalism's reign,

I aimed to disrupt, to break every chain.

Amidst boardrooms of suits and profit margins' flight,

I sought to champion a new, ethical light.

To challenge the norms, to make a difference profound,

In the heart of corporate landscapes, I was bound.

With innovation as my shield and purpose as my guide,

I embarked on a mission, side by side.

To redefine success, not just in monetary gain,

But in values, ethics, and a higher terrain.

In this realm where capitalism's grip was strong,

I aimed to prove that doing right wasn't wrong.

To break the chains of greed and exploitation's hold,

In my pursuit of a future, more equitable and bold.

Through challenges aplenty, I marched ahead,

With a vision of a corporate world better led.

In this surreal landscape where ideals would reign,

I was determined to disrupt and break every chain.

Chapter 3

The Enigma of Corporate Identity

The narrator's questions about why he is different

In DataCorp Tower, where holograms gleam,
A curious dream, a surreal scene,
My mind explores, in surreal delight,
This corporate world, bathed in biz-speak's tight.

The walls transform, an augmented guise,
From virtual realms to dreams that rise.
In this maze of corporate haze,
Questions of self in my mind's ablaze.

"Why do I wander, a lone entity,
While others align with corporate glee?"
I ponder amidst the barcode's trance,
Executives with data's relentless dance.

A VR tiger, a creator of code,
In a binary suit, down the halls he strode,
Reciting market trends, poetic and grand,
In a language that flows like shifting sand.

Amidst the riddles of blockchain's scheme,
I yearn for a unique dream,
But thoughts morph swiftly, data's cascade,
Through predictive corridors, my mind swayed.

In this biz-speak domain, I venture on,
In search of self, to break the chain.
In a world where ROI is the cherished phrase,
I seek my own unique maze.

I dive into the buzzword ocean deep,
Where value propositions and targets creep.
Through fiscal quarters and balance sheets' haze,
I seek authenticity in a corporate craze.

Amidst the corridors of financial might,
I yearn for purpose, to shed the blinding light,
Of profits alone, and embrace a broader view,
Where meaning and impact in harmony grew.

In this realm where bottom lines are king,
I aim to find my own unique wing,
To soar above metrics and corporate praise,
And chart a course through a different maze.

With courage in my heart and a purpose in my stride,
I venture forth, on a unique corporate ride.
In a world where ROI holds a dominant gaze,
I seek my path, in my own distinctive ways.

Chapter 4

Pixelated Lament

The narrator's feelings of alienation and isolation

In TechnoMetropolis, where pixels gleam,
A tale unfolds, a surreal dream.
My thoughts in shadows hide,
In a world of isolation, where I quietly slide.

In pixelated cafes, AI serves the brew,
As emotions dance to jargon's eerie cue.
"Why am I an API, without integration's grace,
In this network of avatars, lost in this digital space?"

I muse amidst coworkers, turned chatbots cold,
Automation's embrace, my stories untold.
A neon sign above, in code it did boast,
"Connection Lost," a digital ghost.

In this bewildering realm, I yearn for the sky,
To break free from algorithms, where personas lie.
To be a disruptor, to bridge the divide,
In a world of masks, where my true self I'd hide.

But words transform into glitchy art,
Emojis and emoticons, a language apart.
Lost in the binary, a void I explore,
In this surreal dystopia, my loneliness soars.

I venture on, a solitary quest,

In a landscape of blockchain trust, I'll be the best.

To connect on a human level, amidst digital's reign,

In "Pixelated Lament," I'll break the chain.

Through lines of code and cryptographic might,

I aim to bridge the gap, bring humanity to light.

In the era of smart contracts and tokens' domain,

I yearn to show that empathy can still reign.

As the world trades data like currency prized,

I see an opportunity, not to be disguised,

To infuse compassion in a tech-driven lane,

In "Pixelated Lament," I'll break the chain.

For amidst the digital streams and data's allure,

I believe in connections that are genuine and pure.

In a world where algorithms aim to constrain,

I'll be the voice of empathy, a heartfelt refrain.

Through decentralized networks and pixels that gleam,

I'll weave threads of humanity into the digital dream.

In a realm of virtuality, where emotions should reign,

In "Pixelated Lament," I'll break the chain.

Chapter 5

The Unicorn's Solitude

The narrator's feeling of not belonging anywhere

In Silicon Citadel's labyrinthine maze,

A tale unfolds in a surreal daze.

My mind, a deepening dive,

An outsider's plight, in the tech elite's hive.

Holographic unicorns roam with grace,

Drones serve IPOs, an impressive chase.

But I grapple with an inner strife,

In the world of tech, a disconnect rife.

"Why am I the bug, an outlier's call,

In this unicorn herd, I stand small?"

I whisper amid colleagues, connected minds,

Neural interfaces weaving, with digital binds.

A door in VR, labeled "Belonging" stood,

Locked behind conformity, as I understood.

In this bewildering world, I seek the key,

To decrypt isolation, to set my soul free.

To disrupt the paradigm, to find my own way,

Amidst startup unicorns, where authenticity may sway.

But as I bridge the digital chasm's tide,

Words turn to code, in the virtual void I ride.

I venture in the techno-society's fold,
Seeking my place, a story untold.
In a landscape of innovation, where language takes flight,
"The Unicorn's Solitude," my journey into the night.

Amid neon streets where holograms swirl,
I ponder my role in this digital world.
The unicorn symbolizing uniqueness and grace,
In a realm where conformity I'd need to face.

Innovation buzzes, a symphony of change,
Yet solitude and individuality feel strange.
In the midst of the crowd, I embark on this flight,
"The Unicorn's Solitude," my quest for what's right.

Through the pixels and screens of a high-tech domain,
I aim to show that uniqueness needn't wane.
In a society of trends and a world colored bright,
"The Unicorn's Solitude," a beacon of light.

For amidst the digital noise and trends of the day,
I believe that individuality will find its way.
In a world of innovation and progress so tight,
"The Unicorn's Solitude," a tale of unique might.

In the techno-society's ever-evolving mold,
I seek to be genuine, courageous, and bold.
In a story where solitude leads to insight,
"The Unicorn's Solitude," my journey through the night.

Chapter 6

The Encryption of Connection

The narrator's difficulty connecting with others

In Biztopia's circuits, where lines did weave,
A tale of connection my heart did conceive,
In a world where jargon was the common tongue,
My quest for kinship had begun.

In holographic events, avatars did convene,
Their language memes, a surreal scene.
But amid synergistic talks, my plea,
Was to bridge the gap and truly connect, you see.

"Why does my bandwidth falter in this coded space,
Among conversations in this digital race?"
I pondered, watching colleagues merge in flow,
M&A deals with chatbots, a surreal techno show.

An AI dove with olive branch, pixelated and bright,
Symbolizing unity in this digital flight.
Yet, the disconnect lingered, a firewall I must break,
To shatter isolation, for humanity's sake.

My words became encrypted, lost in the din,
Of virtual noise, where connections grew thin.
But undeterred, I journeyed, my goal in sight,
To decode human bonds, in this digital light.

In this surreal businesscape, where ROI did reign,
I sought heartfelt connections, to ease the pain.
"The Encryption of Connection," my unwavering theme,
In a world of data streams, where reality's not what it seems.

Amidst boardroom meetings and digital clutter,
I yearned for connections that made hearts flutter.
In the maze of algorithms and financial schemes,
"The Encryption of Connection," my cherished dreams.

For in a world driven by numbers and charts,
I believed genuine relationships held the real smarts.
In this landscape where data flowed like streams,
"The Encryption of Connection," the essence of my dreams.

Through binary codes and virtual interfaces,
I aimed to unveil authentic human embraces.
In a narrative where reality's not what it seems,
"The Encryption of Connection," my beacon of gleams.

In this surreal businesscape, where ROI did reign,
I stood for a truth that would not wane.
In a digital world where reality's not what it seems,
"The Encryption of Connection," my pursuit of genuine themes.

Chapter 7

The Node of Uniqueness

The narrator's feeling of being different from everyone else

In Silicon Synapse City's catacombs deep,

A tale unfolds, where narratives sweep.

My quest, surreal and grand,

In a landscape of conformity, I take my stand.

In holographic calls, avatars converse,

Discussing strategies, in a digital universe.

But I feel distinct, in this peculiar space,

A node decentralized, in the collective's embrace.

"Why am I the outlier, decentralized and free,

In a network of centralized thinking?" I wonder, you see,

As colleagues merge, in AI's consciousness stream,

PowerPoint presentations, the norm of this dream.

A neon sign above, in a language unique,

Spells "Innovation," in zeros and ones, so sleek.

In this bewildering realm, I seek to disrupt,

The status quo's grip, uniqueness I'll erupt.

But thoughts transform, like encrypted streams,

In circuits surreal, in digital dreams.

Through the techscape I venture, the protagonist bold,

In search of my place, where stories are told.

In this world of transformation, where digital does dance,
I aim to stand out, to take a chance.
To embrace individuality, in a landscape so vast,
"The Node of Uniqueness," my journey's steadfast contrast.

In a realm where algorithms run the show,
I seek to break free, let my true self glow.
Amidst data-driven dreams and metrics amassed,
"The Node of Uniqueness," my identity steadfast.

With every click and every line of code,
I challenge the norm, break the traditional mode.
In this evolving world, where innovation is unsurpassed,
"The Node of Uniqueness," my anchor at last.

In the sea of conformity, I chart my course,
Fueled by authenticity, a powerful driving force.
In a digital age where sameness is amassed,
"The Node of Uniqueness," my flag held high and fast.

In this world of transformation, where digital does dance,
I dare to be different, to take a stance.
To celebrate individuality, in a landscape so vast,
"The Node of Uniqueness," my journey's steadfast contrast.

Chapter 8

The Quest for Belonging

The narrator's desire to find a place where he feels accepted

In the Corporate Collective's holographic embrace,
A tale unfolds in this surreal space.
My journey, in a world I'd roam,
Searching for a place to call my home.

In co-working spaces, coworkers take a role,
Morphing into personas, data-driven and whole.
I yearned for acceptance's grace,
A place where I'd thrive, in this complex chase.

"Why must I disrupt, in this world so the same,
In scalable sameness, I play a different game?"
I mused and I pondered, in this world I'd know,
Where colleagues merged, in ecosystems' flow.

A neon sign above, with letters so bright,
Spelling "Inclusivity," in blockchain's light.
In this peculiar world, I sought the key,
To unlock acceptance, where I'd truly be.

To disrupt conformity, norms I'd bend,
In a world of trends, I'd stand as a friend.
But words transformed, as code I'd swirl,
In a surreal network, my thoughts did twirl.

My protagonist ventured, with purpose and pride,
In this businessscape, where voices collide.
Seeking my place, in diversity's domain,
"The Quest for Belonging," my journey's refrain.

In a world where differences often set the tone,
I champion unity, a melody all my own.
Amidst the cacophony of opinions and disdain,
"The Quest for Belonging," my unwavering campaign.

With each step I take, I aim to ignite,
A sense of togetherness, shining so bright.
In a landscape diverse, where cultures entertain,
"The Quest for Belonging," my heartfelt, earnest strain.

Through conversations and bridges I'll build,
Breaking down barriers, my purpose fulfilled.
In a world where division could often reign,
"The Quest for Belonging," my harmonious terrain.

My journey continues, with each chapter's page,
In the quest for belonging, I'll set the stage.
In a corporate world, where connections sustain,
"The Quest for Belonging," my heartfelt, enduring chain.

Chapter 9

Through the Technoscape

The narrator's fear of being alone

Through the technoscape I journeyed, a protagonist so bold,
To conquer fear, escape the chains, of isolation's hold.
In a landscape speaking collaboration's song,
I battled digital solitude, finding where I truly belong.

Amidst virtual meetings and pixels that gleam,
I searched for the essence of a team.
In a world where avatars often replaced a face,
I aimed for genuine connection, in this digital space.

Through the labyrinth of screens, I wove a thread,
A tapestry of bonds, where human connection led.
In a business world where isolation could be strong,
I sought the antidote, where I truly belong.

My journey was a testament to resilience and grace,
In the face of virtual walls, I'd find my place.
In a digital realm, where connection could be so wrong,
I discovered the magic of where I truly belong.

Chapter 10

The Quest for Connection

The narrator's hope of finding a sense of community

In Marketopia's megalopolis, vast and bright,
A tale unfolds amidst holographic light.
My journey, surreal and wide,
Towards a sense of community, where hearts would glide.

In town squares holographic, avatars amassed,
For TED Talks and blockchain, where knowledge was cast.
I dreamt of a tribe, a kin,
A place where I'd find belonging within.

"Could I be the catalyst, a spark so bright,
In fragmented connections, unite the light?"
I wondered, and I pondered, in this digital domain,
Where colleagues merged in visions, like a boundless chain.

A holographic rainbow in the sky did bloom,
Unity in ideas, dispelling the gloom.
In this enigmatic realm, I sought to decode,
Genuine belonging, on this hopeful road.

To disrupt isolation, and nurture connection's grace,
In a world of collaboration, I'd find my place.
Words transformed, like data streams in flow,
Through the surreal network, my hope would grow.

I ventured forth, with courage and might,

In the businessscape surreal, where ideas took flight.

My quest for connection, in this vibrant collection,

"The Quest for Connection," my hopeful reflection.

Amidst virtual meetings and digital tide,

I sought to bridge gaps, far and wide.

In a world where screens often kept me apart,

I yearned for the warmth of a human heart.

Through the web of networks and data's might,

I championed real bonds, shining bright.

In a corporate realm where isolation could be strong,

I believed in the power of connections, all along.

My journey was a testament to hope's ignition,

In a world of screens, I sought real connection.

In this book of stories, my narrative's affection,

"The Quest for Connection," a heartfelt collection.

Chapter 11

The Quest for Acceptance in Technotopia

The narrator's fear of being judged or misunderstood

In Technotopia's shifting maze, my fear did blaze,
In surreal realms of biz-jargon's haze,
a darker path, a haunting craze.
Holographic theaters in the fray,
where pitches to algorithms play,
Judgment's specter held its sway,
in this world, where I'd stray.

"Why am I the beta in this zone,
in a world where final's widely known?
Obsessed with polish, they're overblown,
while I seek acceptance, alone."
I pondered as coworkers swayed,
under virtual scrutiny displayed,
Reputations as assets weighed,
in this realm where all obeyed.

A neon sign in binary's chore,
spelling "Acceptance" on the floor,
Flickered, wavered, and danced galore,
guiding dreams, my heart did implore.
In this perplexing, cryptic land,
misunderstood by the binary band,
I feared the label, the judgment's hand,
the disruptor, not what I'd planned.

As fear took hold, encrypted and cold,
my words in the data sea scrolled,
Lost in virtual tides, I was told,
acceptance sought, yet the path untold.
Through this techscape I'd wade,
determination wouldn't fade,
Seeking acceptance, unafraid,
where innovation's language played.

In Technotopia's shifting tide,
I sought a place to stand with pride,
Amidst the jargon, far and wide,
to be accepted, not pushed aside.

In this world of innovation's race,
I embraced diversity's embrace,
My goal was clear, my path was traced,
to find belonging in that space.

Through coding lines and digital screens,
I sought to bridge those in-betweens,
Inclusion was my cherished means,
in Technotopia's vibrant scenes.

I knew that unity was the key, in this land of tech's esprit,
My journey's goal, for all to see, to find my place in harmony.
In this tech-driven landscape, I would shine,
Embracing differences, forming a line,
In "The Quest for Belonging," my journey's theme,
To find acceptance, in a digital dream.

Chapter 12

Echoes in the Digital Citadel

The narrator's fear of being abandoned

In the holographic corridors, a tale profound,
In the Digital Citadel, a surreal realm unwound.
My journey continued, fear in my chest,
Abandonment's shadow, in this landscape so perplexed.

In a virtual marketplace, where data was the gold,
Colleagues bartered fiercely, in this world, I was bold.
I stood there, feeling somewhat resigned,
As mergers of chatbots left me far behind.

"Why, oh why, the legacy, in a world so fast-paced,
Continuous updates, in this digital race?"
I pondered aloud, with a heart full of strife,
As colleagues moved forward in the rhythm of life.

Loyalty measured by subscriptions, I found,
In a realm of innovation, where change did abound.
A holographic clock, with its relentless chime,
Symbolized the passage of time in this paradigm.

I dreaded the prospect of becoming obsolete,
My contributions fading, a bitter defeat.
Words turned to code, in a virtual domain,
As I faced the fear of being left in disdain.

Yet onward I ventured, with hope in my heart,
To conquer the fear, to play my own part.
In a world of disruption, I sought to define,
The enduring connections that outlasted time.

Through pixelated storms and data's might,
I braved the challenges with all my might.
In "The Quest for Connection," my purpose unwavering,
To find the ties that were truly worth savoring.

I knew that in this digital age,
Real connections weren't just a stage.
In every chat and virtual call,
I aimed to build bonds that wouldn't fall.

Through tech's upheavals and constant change,
I believed that some things could rearrange.
In "The Quest for Connection," my journey's creed,
To find true friendships in this digital need.

Chapter 13

Echoes in the Neon Labyrinth

The narrator's fear of being alone

In the neon-lit corridors, a tale takes a twist,
Corporate Metropolis, where surreal realms persist.
My journey, a haunting refrain,
Fear of abandonment, in the business jargon's domain.

In a holographic boardroom, avatars convene,
Brokered deals with handshakes, an enigmatic scene.
Left behind, I pondered, a legacy to bear,
In a world of innovation, where change was in the air.

"Why am I a protocol of old, in this chase so wild?
Scalability and progress, for every woman and child?"
I questioned the world, as the upgrades did persist,
Loyalty measured in sprints, in this corporate tryst.

Above me, an hourglass, its sands slipping away,
Symbolizing progress, in this relentless day.
I dreaded obsolescence, fading in this show,
As the digital world moved on, leaving me in woe.

My words turned to code, in the digital terrain,
Disappearing slowly, in the corporate rain.
But onward I ventured, through this surreal strife,
Conquering the fear of abandonment, embracing the legacy of life.

In "The Encryption of Connection," I will persist,
To decode the bonds, that couldn't be missed.
In a world where algorithms try to obscure,
I'm determined to find friendships that will endure.

Through pixels and screens, I forge ahead,
Seeking the connections I had always dreaded.
In "The Encryption of Connection," my guiding star,
To find real relationships, no matter how bizarre.

The corporate world may be a maze of disguise,
But I'm determined to unveil the ties.
In "The Encryption of Connection," my mission held,
To reveal the truth, and let genuine bonds be upheld.

Chapter 14

The Quest for Data's Deepest Meaning

The narrator's search for meaning and understanding

In Datastream City's ethereal embrace,
A surreal journey unfolds, a cryptic chase.
I seek wisdom in jargon's disguise,
In the depths of understanding, where knowledge lies.

In a virtual agora, dialogues take flight,
Deep learning symposiums, an AI's insight.
Comprehension my quest, an insatiable desire,
In this interconnected sea, where data sets inspire.

"Why the outlier am I, amidst this vast array?
Interconnected data, in a grand data ballet."
I ponder the world, my thirst never to cease,
In this search for enlightenment, where data found its release.

A holographic oracle, whispers profound,
"Cascading enlightenment," in data's mystic sound.
To decode existence, my purpose defined,
Disrupting confusion in a knowledge-inclined mind.

Words morphed to networks, in the surreal data's domain,
A quest for understanding, knowledge to attain.
Through the surreal technoscape, I venture to explore,
Unlocking the universe's wisdom, forever seeking more.

In "Binary Echoes," I embarked on a quest,

In search of the answers, on a knowledge conquest.

Through corridors of algorithms, I bravely strode,

In this Wonderland of business, seeking something bold.

Numbers became the language, in which I conversed,

In a world where data reigned, and profits were dispersed.

But in "Binary Echoes," I aspired to transcend,

To find the wisdom that data alone couldn't comprehend.

In the surreal landscape of corporate dreams,

I pursued knowledge, or so it seems.

In "Binary Echoes," my journey did swell,

A quest for understanding, where past and future did dwell.

Chapter 15

The Quest for Digital Enlightenment

The narrator's sense of being an outsider

In Datastream City's ethereal domain,

A surreal journey unfolds, in rhyme's sweet refrain.

I seek meaning in business jargon's disguise,

In the depths of comprehension, where knowledge relies.

In a virtual agora, avatars converse with delight,

Deep learning dialogues, a surreal digital flight.

My thirst for wisdom, an insatiable flame,

In this sea of data, where insight's the game.

"Why the outlier am I in this vast data sea?

Interconnected, they flow, like a symphony."

I ponder existence, in this world I explore,

In search of enlightenment, where data's in galore.

A holographic oracle, whispers of profound,

"Enlightenment cascades," in data streams that astound.

To decode existence, my quest shall unfurl,

Disrupting confusion in this data-driven world.

Words morph to networks, in data's intricate guise,

A quest for deep meaning, where insight complies.

Through surreal technoscape, my journey's replete,

Unlocking universe's wisdom, a quest ever sweet.

In "Binary Echoes," I venture anew,

In search of the knowledge, both ancient and true.

Through algorithms and data, I seek to unveil,

The secrets of existence, beyond the corporate veil.

Numbers and codes, in a digital dance,

In the vast expanse of data, I take a chance.

But in "Binary Echoes," my pursuit is clear,

To find profound meaning, to make the vision appear.

In the surreal landscape of corporate wonder,

I delve into data, a journey to ponder.

In "Binary Echoes," my quest takes flight,

A pursuit of wisdom, in the realm of data's light.

Chapter 16

The Quest for Digital Belonging

The narrator's longing to belong

In Cyberopolis, data currents dance,
A surreal journey unfolds, in a mystic trance.
I seek belonging, in jargon's attire,
In the shifting data tides, where I aspire.

In the holographic marketplace, metrics interlace,
Emotions and synergies in a digital space.
My longing for home, a distant star's grace,
In this ecosystem, where connections we chase.

"Why the algorithm adrift in this collaboration sea?
Neural networks converge, yet what about me?"
I ponder in silence, in this world so grand,
Seeking genuine bonds in this virtual land.

A holographic keyhole, a symbol of quest,
For belonging I journey, a hopeful bequest.
Disrupting isolation, in a realm of connection,
Where the language of innovation seeks human reflection.

Words morph to code, in the digital domain,
A quest for my place, in a landscape's refrain.
Through surreal data-scape, I press and I yearn,
For the essence of belonging, in a world's return.

In "The Quest for Belonging," my journey took flight,
In a world of diversity, both day and night.
Amidst voices that clashed, and ideas that did churn,
I sought a connection, a sense of concern.

The bytes and the algorithms, in a symphony combined,
In "The Quest for Belonging," my story entwined.
In the technotopia's shifting stride,
I battled isolation, found where I could reside.

In the landscape of business, where data did swell,
I aimed for acceptance, in this world where I'd dwell.
In "The Quest for Belonging," my hope remained clear,
To find my true place, in a realm far and near.

Chapter 17

The Fear of Digital Rejection

The narrator's fear of being rejected

In the circuits of Silicon Synapse City's grand expanse,
A surreal journey unfolds, in a cryptic dance.
I grapple with rejection's dark decree,
In the labyrinth of tech, where shadows flee.

In the virtual agora, where emotions intertwine,
Contracts and mergers, in a digital design.
"Why the deprecated feature, in this world so vast?
In constant upgrades, will I be the last?"

I ponder in silence, as trends take their toll,
My loyalty measured, in updates of the soul.
A holographic "Decline" in the distance looms,
Symbolizing exclusion, in digital rooms.

The fear of dismissal, of contributions denied,
Labeled as irrelevant, a relentless tide.
My words into code, deprecated and erased,
In the surreal data abyss, I journey, chaste.

I press forward, determined to find the way,
Overcoming rejection, in the light of day.
In this techno-society, where progress we adore,
Legacy and resilience, I seek to restore.

In "The Quest for Acceptance," my journey unfolds,
Amidst pixels and data, where stories are told.
I strive to be seen, not just data to store,
In the annals of business, where dreams I explore.

Through trials and hardships, I battle the tide,
In "The Quest for Acceptance," I walk with pride.
I stand up against indifference's cruel roar,
In the heart of the corporate, where I yearn for more.

With courage and vigor, I venture ahead,
In "The Quest for Acceptance," I'll write my own thread.
In a world of algorithms, where metrics implore,
I'll carve out my space, with determination galore.

Chapter 18

The Quest for Self-Acceptance in Bizmorphic Metropolis

The narrator's struggle to accept himself

In the realm of Bizmorphic Metropolis, surreal and grand,
My odyssey unfolds, in this complex land.
A struggle profound, a quest I must face,
Framed in business jargon's intricate embrace.

In a holographic chamber, self-assessment's decree,
Personal brand strategies, a confounding sea.
"Why the pivot in my tale, a conflict so deep?
Between reinvention and self, secrets to keep?"

I ponder the paradox, a dual nature's dance,
Professional and personal, in one life's expanse.
LinkedIn endorsements, a measure so wide,
In the flickering neon, where identity hides.

In this bewildering world, I seek the grand key,
To decrypt my true self, to set my soul free.
Imposter syndrome's illusion, I aim to disrupt,
In a land where vulnerability they seldom erupt.

As I venture further, on the path I'd embark,
My words turn to binary, a dance in the dark.
Self-doubt as 1s, and self-acceptance as 0s,
In this surreal quest, where authenticity grows.

I persist, in this landscape of lore,
Discovering my true self, I'd search evermore.
In a world of success, where speeches were plenty,
I found that embracing self was the ultimate twenty.

In "The Quest for Self-Discovery," I dared to explore,
Unraveling layers, learning, and growing galore.
I sought out my essence, my heart's inner sentry,
A journey of self-love, pure and elementary.

With each step I took, I uncovered the key,
In "The Quest for Self-Discovery," I learned to be free.
No more chasing illusions, no need to be phony,
I'd walk my own path, guided by self, not baloney.

Through trials and triumphs, I'd find my own grace,
In "The Quest for Self-Discovery," I'd truly embrace,
The person within, the one I adore,
In the vast, surreal landscape, I'd shine even more.

Chapter 19

The Denial of Data in TechnoHealth Nexus

The narrator's initial denial of his sickness

In the data tunnels' labyrinth, my tale unfolds,
In TechnoHealth Nexus, where reality unfolds.
My surreal journey begins, denial at its core,
In business jargon's grasp, a challenge to explore.

Within a virtual ward, avatars play their part,
Exchanging wellness metrics, a diagnostic art.
I cling to the notion, illness I'll defy,
Resisting data-driven truths, in denial I lie.

"Why the firewall 'gainst metrics, my wellness to dismiss,
In this world of diagnoses, something's amiss?"
I wonder amidst colleagues, embracing health's trends,
Real-time analytics, on which their wellness depends.

A holographic thermometer, swings 'tween "Optimal" and "Real,"
Symbolizing my struggle, in a healthcare ordeal.
Denying my vulnerability, I hold data at bay,
Words transformed to obscured data, truth kept away.

In this surreal healthscape, where prevention takes flight,
Confronting my ailment, my inner fight.
In a world of preventive measures, it's sometimes a must,
To acknowledge our frailty, our humanness to trust.

In "The Battle Within," I faced illness so bold,
Navigating the landscape where stories unfold.
My journey was daunting, but I wouldn't be crushed,
In the surreal healthscape, where strength could be hushed.

With resilience as armor, and hope as my guide,
In "The Battle Within," I'd stand strong and wide.
For in facing my ailment, in this uncharted thrust,
I'd discover my courage, in myself, I'd trust.

Through trials and treatments, I'd find a new way,
In "The Battle Within," I'd seize the bright day.
No surrender to sickness, no turning to dust,
In this surreal healthscape, I'd rise from the crust.

Chapter 20

The Awakening in HealthTech Haven

The narrator's gradual acceptance of his sickness

In HealthTech Haven's corridors, my story unfolds,
A surreal journey of acceptance, a tale to behold.
Marked by gradual understanding, of sickness I conceded,
In business jargon's cryptic grasp, a transformative deed.

Within the wellness expo, where avatars exchanged,
Health data and histories, a landscape rearranged.
My resistance began to gently fade,
As understanding grew, my path newly laid.

"Why be the legacy system, clinging to what's past?
In health's own protocol, a die has been cast."
I pondered 'midst colleagues, embracing trends anew,
Vitality measured by tech, as wellness I'd pursue.

A holographic phoenix, rising in the data's trance,
Symbolizing rebirth, in wellness' graceful dance.
Decrypting signs of ailment, I embraced what's real,
Acknowledging vulnerability, a powerful ordeal.

My words transformed into code, a bridge of transformation,
From past denial to acceptance, a newfound dedication.
In this surreal healthscape, resilience found its place,
Confronting my condition, with a determined embrace.

In a world of optimization, where progress took the reign,
I found the strength in self-awareness, a power to sustain.
"The Awakening in HealthTech Haven," my journey's decree,
A tale of transformation, a surreal odyssey.

In a world of optimization, where KPIs and metrics reign,
I found the strength in self-awareness, a power to sustain.
"The Paradigm Shift in HealthTech Haven," my journey's decree,
A tale of transformation, a surreal corporate odyssey.

Amidst ROI goals and stock market kinetics in play,
I navigated the landscape, forging a lucrative way.
In this surreal healthscape, where innovation did plea,
I unlocked potential, a healthtech IPO jubilee.

With strategic pivots and profit projections aligned,
I weathered the market's fluctuations, a path well-defined.
In this corporate realm, where healthtech stocks ran free,
I carved my success story, for all to see.

Chapter 21

The Quest for Assurance in MedTech Metropolis

The narrator's fears and concerns about his sickness

I ventured forth, through introspection's stride,

To confront my deepest fears, on this surreal ride.

In a world of prevention, where health's complexity would enthrall,

"The Quest for Assurance in MedTech Metropolis" would enthrall.

Amidst risk assessments and market evaluations so keen,

I navigated the healthcare arena with a disciplined mien.

In this MedTech realm, where compliance did call,

I sought assurance, a healthcare firewall.

Through policy changes and regulatory dance so wide,

I ensured patient trust in every stride.

In this corporate domain, where health standards stood tall,

I built a legacy, preventing every health pitfall.

With healthcare strategies and growth projections aligned,

I forged a path through the industry, well-defined.

In this surreal landscape, where innovation held its thrall,

I secured assurance, MedTech's protocol.

Chapter 22

Dreams in the Halls of HealthInnovate Utopia

The narrator's hopes and dreams for the future

In HealthInnovate Utopia's interconnected domain,
My surreal journey took flight, with dreams in its rein.
Wrapped in business jargon, mystifying and grand,
I sought hope in this vast healthful land.

Within holographic visions, avatars did convene,
Trading wellness dreams, like a vivid dream scene.
They conducted ROI analyses on life's vital goals,
While I envisioned vibrant, healthful souls.

"Why not be the disruptor in this narrative's thread,
Creating a well-being ecosystem," I said,
A future where health's not just metrics, but a dream,
Where KPIs and wellness merge, in a harmonious stream.

A holographic phoenix, soaring high,
A symbol of transformation in the healthful sky,
In this surreal realm, aspirations took flight,
As dreams painted the path, and hopes burned bright.

My words became streams of visionary grace,
Painting a future, a healthier, brighter place.
In this landscape of wellness, aspirations in a heap,
"Dreams in the Halls of HealthInnovate Utopia" I'd keep.

Amidst market fluctuations and stock values that sway,

I navigated the industry in a strategic way.

In this realm of health innovation, where challenges run deep,

I learned that dreams fueled progress, a secret to keep.

With diligence and metrics, I pursued my vision,

Balancing the bottom line with patient care precision.

In this corporate healthscape, where ROI I'd reap,

I found that dreams could drive success, even when mountains seemed steep.

My journey taught me that in health's grand scheme,

Dreams and innovation were more than they'd seem.

In this surreal health domain, where hope and innovation seep,

I discovered that dreams could make wellness a reality to keep.

Chapter 23

The Train of Cryptic Wisdom

The narrator's confusion and disorientation

Amid the circuits surreal, where data did impress,
My puzzling journey began, in a world of strangeness.
The Information Express, fusion modern and past,
On quantum tracks it rattled, a neon journey vast.

I boarded, met a conductor, whose form was never still,
Shifting suits and personas, a voice with a LinkedIn thrill.
"Welcome to Wisdom's Train," the conductor's words did express,
In echoes of endorsements, a surreal finesse.

My seat, live stock prices, but numbers danced in haste,
Cryptic hieroglyphs emerging, a surrealistic taste.
Outside, a spreadsheet landscape, endless rows did unfurl,
A surreal data vision, a never-ending swirl.

"Why, in this transformation, am I deprecated, it seems?"
I clutched charts and spreadsheets, chasing elusive dreams.
The conductor's face turned emoji, a mix of confusion and jest,
In this surreal train of business, I sought a moment's rest.

My thoughts trapped in a loop, of buzzwords and charts in a spin,
My sense of direction lost in data's chaotic din.
Amid surreal jargon's landscape, I longed for a different tune,
In a world where clarity seemed to wane, like the crescent moon.

Yet I pressed on, navigating through the stock market's ebbs and flows,
Strategically maneuvering in the business realm as complexity grows.
In this surreal corporate world where challenges came and went,
I understood that clarity and vision could be potent.

My journey taught me that the business world isn't just about numbers and trends,
But also about the passions and visions of individuals that can lead to dividends.
In this surreal corporate landscape where words and concepts seemed like code,
I realized that clarity and vision held value as complexity continued to unfold.

Chapter 24

The Corporate Conundrum Express

The narrator's search for meaning and understanding

Amid the labyrinthine tracks of corporate's grand express,
My surreal tale unfolds, where meaning's in excess.
Aboard a shifting carriage, boardrooms in disguise,
Where PowerPoint presentations meet disconnected ties.

"Why am I the outlier in synergy's complex dance,
Lost 'midst buzzwords' chaos, in corporate's vast expanse?"
I pondered 'midst the passengers, in data's metrics sway,
Quantifying every thought, in KPIs' array.

From the train's ceiling, holographic oracle did rise,
Bar charts and trend lines, in its voice, I recognized.
"Optimization" it spoke, and "Value Creation" grand,
In this corporate puzzle, I sought to understand.

In the train, a world surreal, I yearned to find the key,
To decrypt life's mysteries in this corporate odyssey.
My words transformed to data streams, cascading in the air,
In search of deeper meaning, I journeyed through the snare.

Amid this corporate conundrum, I sought to break the spell,
To find true comprehension in this world where numbers swell.
In a land of metrics' mastery, I pursued wisdom's grace,
On the Corporate Conundrum Express, in search of a different place.

I knew the importance of ROI, EBITDA, and P/E ratios,

But I also yearned for insights beyond the balance sheets and flowcharts,

oh! In this surreal stock market ballet, where trends could quickly dispel,

I realized that wisdom's touch could guide me oh so well.

The journey taught me that while data drove decisions with a relentless pace,

True comprehension came from blending knowledge with a human embrace.

In this corporate landscape, where acronyms and analytics could befell,

I learned that wisdom was the compass that led me from the corporate spell.

Chapter 25

The Enigmatic Express of Data Dreamland

The narrator's encounters with other people

In Data Dreamland's depths, the corporate train did glide,
A tale of strange encounters, where jargon's in the tide.
A woman with stock tickers, her face a market's spin,
Conversing in graphs and codes, her world, a digital din.

"Let's leverage synergies," she said, her eyes like pie charts turned,
In this surreal carriage, where profit's fire burned.
Further down, an office printer-man, spreadsheets in his head,
Maximizing ROI, his tie a waterfall's thread.

Consultants in holographic form, brainstormed in the air,
Flowcharts filled the space, creating quite a flair.
"Our insights actionable," they chanted with a grin,
In this world of metrics' tongue, my journey did begin.

I sought connections, 'midst this jargon's haze,
My words turned to data clouds, attempting in a maze.
In this surreal Data Dreamland, where efficiency's the song,
I delved into these mysteries, where the corporate train sped along.

In a world of cryptic language, beneath each business mask,
I searched for human essence, in this enigmatic task.
A journey through surrealness, where efficiency's but a screen,
On the Enigmatic Express, where meanings lie between.

I navigated through the jargon, the IPOs and M&As,
But beneath the market movements, I sought more than a phase.
In this corporate riddle's embrace, where profit's often seen,
I yearned for deeper insights, where the soul could intervene.

The Enigmatic Express carried me through the maze of stock and trade,
But my quest for authenticity was a path less often laid.
In this surreal marketplace, where algorithms often convene,
I discovered the enigmatic truths that lay beyond the screen.

Chapter 26

The Relic of Data Dreamland

The narrator's discovery of the old factory

Through the digital wilderness, the train did swiftly glide,
In Data Dreamland's landscape, where jargon's in the tide.
But on the outskirts, a factory stood, an old and ghostly scene,
A relic of a bygone age, where things were once more plain.

"Legacy Manufacturing Co.," the sign said with a glitchy flair,
In this surreal setting, free from digital's snare.
Machinery, cubicles, typewriters, all covered in a shroud,
A place untouched by business speak, where authenticity was allowed.

"Why does this place feel like a refuge in this jargon's noisy din?"
I wondered in the quiet of the factory's din.
In plain language, old files spoke, of humans,
Not machines, Amidst the train's complexity, simplicity's beauty gleams.

In this surreal factory, understanding found its birth,
The value of human connection in the vast expanse of earth.
My words turned into letters, expressing newfound grace,
Balancing business's efficiency with the old world's warm embrace.

The journey now transformed, as train and factory intertwined,
In "The Relic of Data Dreamland," a lesson for mankind.
To balance progress with simplicity, where all our hearts can land,
In the landscape of the future, hand in hand with what's unplanned.

The journey now transformed, as train and factory intertwined,
In "The Relic of Data Dreamland," a lesson for humankind.
In this merger of efficiency and human touch so grand,
I found the key to harmony, where innovation could expand.

Amidst the KPIs and bottom lines, I grasped a truth so deep,
In the midst of business jargon, where contracts often creep.
"The Relic of Data Dreamland" spoke of balance and demand,
To embrace technology's advance, while keeping hearts in hand.

Through stock market storms and digital streams, steered with steady hand,
In this corporate quest for progress, where every gain was planned.
"The Relic of Data Dreamland" showed a path to understand,
That innovation with compassion can flourish, a truly timeless brand.

Chapter 27

The Factory of Echoing Whirrs

The narrator's initial impression of the factory

In Data Dreamland's twilight, a surreal place to be,
The Factory of Echoing Whirrs, a sight for all to see.
Its chrome and glass did shimmer, with holographic grace,
A structure vast and innovative, in a mystifying space.

The entrance beckoned forward, with interconnected gears,
A world of constant progress, innovation through the years.
"Why am I the beta tester?" I did inquire,
In this land of aspirations, where innovation was on fire.

Robots danced in harmony, orchestrating with precision,
A mesmerizing spectacle, sparking creative vision.
A neon sign above them, "Productivity" it read,
In cascading numbers' glow, ideas were born and bred.

Within this surreal setting, where progress held its reign,
My words transformed, to decode the factory's gain.
I ventured forth with purpose, the secrets to unfurl,
In a world of innovation, where journeys make us twirl.

Amidst the business models, I sought the factory's heart,
To understand its essence, and play my destined part.
With newfound clarity, my insights did unfurl,
Beyond the metrics' sway, a vision's gentle swirl.

Chapter 28

The Labyrinth of Whirling Illusions

The narrator's sense of confusion and disorientation

Within the Factory of Echoing Whirrs, a maze of grand design,
My journey twisted, in a world most asinine.
Holographic charts hung mid-air, an ever-looping spree,
Conveyor belts of presentations, a visual cacophony.

"Am I an error code?" I asked, amidst illusions grand,
In this cascade of data's dance, across the shifting land.
Signposts pointed every way, each path with different aims,
The architecture challenged minds, immersed in data's games.

In this bewildering surreal land, where logic came undone,
My words turned into scrambled code, in this labyrinth I'd run.
Determined to find clarity, 'midst the chaos that unfurled,
In a world of grand illusions, where understanding was the pearl.

Amidst the market fluctuations and stock prices' wild sway,
I sought to decipher patterns in the data every day.
In "The Code of Market Mirage," a story worth the whirl,
A lesson in financial wisdom, where knowledge was the pearl.

Chapter 29

The Quest for the Red Handbag's Algorithm

The narrator's search for the woman in the red handbag

Deep in the Factory of Echoing Whirrs, a quest did unfurl,
My search for a woman in red, in this surreal business world.
Whispers of her held the key, to secrets yet concealed,
An algorithm for success, the ultimate data revealed.

"Why's she the enigma here," I mused, in jargon's grip I swirled,
Holographic clues in hand, in this coded labyrinth I twirled.
Opportunity flickered above, in symbols mystified,
The quest for insight and the truth, my purpose amplified.

In this technoscape surreal, I followed trails of data's gleam,
My words became encrypted streams, like fragments of a dream.
Determined to unveil her secrets, in this landscape I'd progress,
Where innovation's language flowed, but human touch held success.

Amidst the blockchain's ledger, and the cryptocurrency's spin,
I aimed to decrypt the future, find the code that lay within.
In "The Enigma of Digital Gold," where digital fortunes impress,
A tale of crypto wisdom, where transparency was success.

Chapter 30

The Resonance of Relic Works

The narrator's discovery of the old factory

Deep within the digital's complex tides,
I unveiled a discovery, where the past resides.
A factory forgotten, "The Relic Works" in name,
Amidst corporate algorithms, its existence came.

Machines of yore in slumber deep,
Analog dreams in cobwebs to keep.
Typewriters sang a clunky, nostalgic song,
As analog clocks chimed, where time felt strong.

"Why's this place a time warp?" I thought, amazed,
'Midst the relics of history, I stood, quite dazed.
A neon sign flickered, "Innovation and History's balm,"
A paradoxical haven, a surreal healing psalm.

Amidst the confusion, wonder did unfurl,
In a world of progress, nostalgia's pearl.
The blend of history and innovation, I found,
In "The Relic Works," where past's echoes abound.

My words transformed into letters, handwritten and true,
A journey of balance, of the old and the new.
In a landscape of advancement, I sought to see,
The beauty of tradition and deep humanity.

I pressed forward, navigating this duality,

In "The Relic Works," I found my reality.

A quest for meaning, where past and present kissed,

In a story surreal, through time's mystic twist.

I pressed forward, navigating duality's maze,

In "The Relic Works," I found my reality's gaze.

A quest for meaning, where past and present kissed,

In a surreal story, through time's mystic mist.

Amidst the stock market's fluctuations and the corporate haze,

I sought the essence of value, in this complex maze.

In "The Market Alchemy," where fortunes would persist,

A tale of investment wisdom, where insight couldn't be missed.

Chapter 31

Binary Echoes

The narrator's thoughts and feelings about the factory

I pressed forward, on this journey to dwell,
In "Binary Echoes," where past and future did swell.
A quest for understanding, in a world of progress and old,
A tale surreal, where echoes of time unfold.

I ventured through the corridors of data's embrace,
In search of wisdom that transcended time and space.
Past whispers of legacy systems and ancient code,
I sought the knowledge that had not eroded.

In "Binary Echoes," where lines of code had a voice,
I uncovered secrets that made my heart rejoice.
The past spoke of lessons, the future held dreams,
In this surreal narrative, where nothing was as it seems.

Through the algorithmic haze, I forged my path,
Unraveling mysteries, escaping the digital wrath.
In the echoes of binary, past and future did blend,
A journey of discovery, with no clear end.

So onward I traveled, through this data-driven realm,
In "Binary Echoes," where narratives overwhelm.
A quest for enlightenment, in a world both new and old,
A tale of persistence, where echoes of time unfold.

Chapter 32

Echoes of Binary Time: Past, Present, and Future Unbound

The narrator's confusion and disorientation

Amidst mechanical marvels, a factory's intrigue,
My journey unfolded, surreal and unique.
In "Binary Echoes," bewildering, I'd learn,
In a mystifying world where jargon did churn.

Antique chambers, where gears met with streams,
A baffling confluence, a world of strange dreams.
Ledgers transformed to virtual sheets that I'd see,
As analog ticked on with timestamps in spree.

"Why, in this maze, am I a relic in code?"
I questioned aloud, in the factory's abode.
A neon sign flickered, between times it would swing,
Past and Future entwined, a perplexing thing.

In this mystifying realm, my understanding did blur,
Analog past and digital future would inter.
My words became data, encrypted and vast,
Reflecting the chaos that left me aghast.

Yet forward I pressed, in the journey I'd roam,
To find clarity amidst chaos, I'd comb.
A landscape surreal, with lessons profound,
Where the past met the present, and future unbound.

In the world of business, where mergers and deals align,
I sought answers amidst stock charts that did entwine.
In "The Convergence of Finance," where fortunes were wound,
A narrative of corporate strategy, where wisdom was found.

Through the corridors of analysis and strategies so keen,
I ventured, in "The Analytical Maze," the data-driven scene.
A quest for insights, where numbers did astound,
A story of financial mastery, where knowledge would abound.

Chapter 33

Chronicles of the Red Handbag: Navigating Time's Enigma

The narrator's search for the woman in the red handbag

In the Old Factory of Binary Echoes, a tale does unfurl,
A surreal journey in a temporal swirl.
I seek a woman with a red handbag in tow,
Amidst business jargon's perplexing flow.

Legends whispered by spectral apparitions grand,
Of a cipher with secrets and wisdom to understand.
Her briefcase, they said, holds knowledge untold,
Of past and of future, its mysteries unfold.

"Why am I the key in this time's enigmatic spree?"
I pondered, sought answers to see.
My silhouette woven with threads of the ages past,
A sign overhead, a paradox cast.

In this mystifying realm, a quest does begin,
Exploration in language where epochs do spin.
Words transformed to data, encrypted in code,
I follow breadcrumbs, in time's ebb and flow.

With determination, I roam,
Unveiling the secrets of temporal's home.
In a surreal landscape, where innovation does rhyme,
Yet missed lessons profound, lost in the sands of time.

In the realm of corporations, where strategies take flight,
I aim to decipher the trends, in "Strategic Insights."
A journey through the market, where fluctuations unwind,
A tale of business acumen, where success I'd find.

Through the passages of investments, where assets do grow,
In "The Portfolio Paradox," I venture to know.
A quest for wealth's essence, where fortunes do climb,
A narrative of financial wisdom, in the world so prime.

In the realm of financial markets, where stocks rise and fall,
I seek to understand the rhythm, in "Market's Call."
A journey through volatility, where insights do chime,
A story of stock market mastery, where wealth I'd prime.

Chapter 34

Harmony of Time: The Old Factory's Dichotomy

The narrator's discovery of the old factory

In Data Dreamland's ever-shifting scene,
I embark on a surreal journey, a world in-between.
A discovery awaits, hidden from sight,
The Old Factory of Analog's mystic light.

Holographic banners proclaim and spin,
"Legacy" and "Innovation," a dance begun.
A realm of contradiction,
defying decree, Beta testing life's dichotomy.

"Why the enigma in this fusion so bold?"
I wonder, in stories untold.
Gears merge with rust, a fusion so strange,
A sign toggles between "Tradition" and "Change."

Within, typewriters whisper in digital code,
Analog clocks dance where data streams flow.
Anachronistic marvels, a blend of the past,
Challenge my grasp, a riddle amassed.

In this perplexing realm, words play a game,
Of past and future, analog's name.
Transformed into streams of encrypted grace,
Reflecting the challenge of this surreal space.

Undeterred, I seek to unfold,
The secrets and mysteries this factory holds.
In a landscape of voices that chant innovation's plea,
I uncover the lessons in this dichotomy.

Through the maze of supply chains, where efficiency's revered,
In "Supply Chain Symphony," I persevered.
A quest for streamlined processes, where profits align,
A narrative of logistics expertise, in this corporate design.

In the world of mergers, where corporations unite,
I delved into the complexities, in "Mergers' Flight."
A journey through acquisition, where strategies entwine,
A story of corporate synergy, where fortunes combine.

In the realm of entrepreneurship, where startups take flight,
I explored the challenges faced, in "Startup's Bite."
A quest for innovation's essence, where risks intertwine,
A narrative of entrepreneurial spirit, where my dreams I'd refine.

In the domain of technology, where innovation's the key,
I ventured into "Techtonic Shift," with curiosity.
A journey through digital transformation, where boundaries realign,
A tale of tech disruption, where the future does shine.

In the world of corporate giants, where power does prevail, I
 probed the dynamics of "Titan's Trail."
A quest for market dominance, where strategies intertwine,
A story of corporate ambition, where my success I'd define.

Through the intricate web of globalization's call,

In "Globalization's Labyrinth," I explored it all.

A journey through international markets, where cultures combine,

A narrative of global business, where connections I'd refine.

Undeterred, I pressed forward, in this corporate quest,

Unraveling the mysteries, putting my skills to the test.

In a world of business complexities, where insights entwine,

I sought the essence of success, where my star would shine.

Chapter 35

Echoes of Solitude in the Analog Abyss

The Narrator's Sense of Alienation and Isolation

In this world of gears and holograms, surreal and deep,
I wander the Old Factory, lost in its maze.
Alienation's siren song echoes in my heart,
As I search for my place in this strange new place.

Mechanical relics and holographic streams swirl around me,
A paradoxical embrace of past and future. I see
myself reflected in the factory's gaze,
My own disconnection mirrored in its maze.

"Why this legacy role in a world so profound,
Where past and future are forever bound?"
I murmur in anguish, lost in the game,
As the neon sign swings, Integration and Solitude's name.

In this bewildering world, isolation blooms,
A chasm so wide, a deep sense of gloom.
I yearn for connection, for bridges to build,
My words turning to code, with longing fulfilled.

Onward I venture, through this factory's domain,
Where tradition meets progress, where worlds constrain.
In search of a solace, a genuine connection I'll be,
In a landscape that speaks of connectivity's sea.

Amid the assembly lines, where efficiency is the song,
In "Assembly of Insights," I journey along.
A quest for optimization, where data points align,
A narrative of operational excellence, where efficiency I'll define.

In the world of corporate culture, where values hold sway,
I explore the dynamics in "Culture's Array."
A journey through organizational ethos, where beliefs intertwine,
A story of workplace harmony, where culture I'll refine.

In the realm of leadership, where visionaries reside,
I delve into the essence of "Leadership's Guide."
A quest for effective guidance, where strategies entwine,
A narrative of inspirational leadership, where success does shine.

In the domain of customer service, where satisfaction's the key,
I venture into "Customer's Symphony," with glee.
A journey through client relations, where needs align,
A tale of exemplary service, where customer loyalty I'll define.

In the world of ethical dilemmas, where choices prevail,
I ponder the intricacies in "Ethics' Scale."
A quest for moral compass, where values intertwine,
A story of ethical decision-making, where integrity I'll refine.

Through the intricate web of teamwork's embrace,
In "Teamwork's Odyssey," I find my place.
A journey through collaboration, where strengths align,
A narrative of cooperative synergy, where bonds I'll redefine.

Chapter 36

The Quest for Meaning in the Code of Existence

The narrator's search for purpose and direction

In TechnoExistence City, where data streams unfurled,
I embarked on a quest through a complex world.
A journey surreal, where meaning lay concealed,
In business jargon's labyrinth, my fate was sealed.

In holographic squares, where avatars conversed,
Philosophical algorithms, life's questions immersed.
I pondered my purpose, feeling out of sync,
Lost in a world of ROI, where purpose could shrink.

"Why a deprecated function in this grand design?
Lost in the hunt for profit, in a world so inclined?"
I mused with frustration, in a world full of strife,
Where "Purpose" and "Profit" swung like the pendulum of life.

In this surreal realm, I embarked on my quest,
To decrypt the meaning, to be different from the rest.
My words turned to data, pondering existence's lore,
In a city where success often left me wanting more.

Forward I pressed, through the digital sprawl,
In search of my purpose, I questioned it all.
In a world of success, where the journey was key,
I yearned for the meaning, for a life that felt free.

In TechnoExistence City, where data ebbed and flowed,
The quest for life's meaning was the path I chose to go.
In the language of business, I sought the profound,
To understand existence, in a world so tightly wound.

In TechnoExistence City, where data ebbed and flowed,
The quest for life's meaning was the path I chose to go.
In the language of business, ROI's rule was profound,
I aimed to decode existence, in a world so tightly wound.

Amidst the stock market's tumult, where shares rose and fell,
I contemplated life's value in "Marketplace's Spell."
A journey through financial landscapes, where numbers align,
A story of wealth and purpose, where investments I'd define.

In the realm of competition, where rivals fought the fight,
I explored life's challenges in "Competition's Light."
A quest for success and survival, where strategies entwine,
A narrative of resilience, where ambition I'd refine.

Through the corporate ladder's rungs, where hierarchies stand tall,
I pondered life's climb in "Hierarchy's Call."
A journey through career progression, where ambitions align,
A tale of aspirations and advancement, where success I'd define.

In the domain of innovation, where ideas took flight,
I delved into existence in "Innovation's Sight."
A quest for creativity and change, where visions entwine,
A story of invention and transformation, where progress I'd define.

In the realm of investments, where fortunes were sought,
I ventured into "Investor's Thought" with thought.
A journey through financial strategies, where goals align,
A narrative of wealth and wisdom, where prosperity I'd define.

Onward I pressed, in my quest for life's core,
Finding wisdom in business's language, seeking meaning galore.
In a world of numbers and strategies, where insights entwine,
I explored the essence of existence, where purpose would shine.

Chapter 37

The Quest for Certainty in the Ambiguity of Existence

The narrator's doubts and uncertainties

In TechnoExistence City, where data streams flow,
I embarked on a journey, a quest to bestow,
Meaning upon life in this surreal digital sprawl,
But doubts and uncertainties began to enthrall.

In a virtual amphitheater, debates filled the air,
Existential quandaries, a complex affair.
SWOT analyses conducted on life's many choices,
My inner struggle raised haunting voices.

"Why the outdated algorithm in this search for life's grace,
Plagued by doubts and risks in this vast digital space?"
I pondered in whispers, as colleagues stood tall,
Achievement metrics measured, my ambitions in thrall.

A neon sign flickered, swung between two extremes,
"Certainty" and "Ambiguity," in the amphitheater's gleams.
In this puzzling realm, doubts grew like a tide,
Casting shadows on purpose, causing me to hide.

My quest for meaning seemed lost in the crowd,
As uncertainty whispered, and my thoughts were unbowed.
My words became data, swirling, uncertain, and vast,
In a city of success, I questioned my path at last.

Yet onward I pressed, through the data's blind maze,

To confront my uncertainties, in a bewildering daze.

In a city that thrived on the language of surety,

I sought courage and clarity in a world so full of obscurity.

In TechnoExistence City, where data never ceased,

The quest for life's meaning was a struggle, a beast.

In a language of business and numbers so plain,

I yearned for assurance in a world full of strain.

In TechnoExistence City, where data never ceased,

The quest for life's meaning was a challenge increased.

In a language of business, where acronyms reign,

I sought assurance in a world marked by strain.

Amidst the stock market's fluctuations, where fortunes did sway,

I pondered existence's value in "Stock Price's Display."

A journey through financial tumult, where investments align,

A tale of wealth and fulfillment, where purpose I'd define.

In the realm of competition, where rivals engaged,

I explored life's hurdles in "Competitive Stage."

A quest for success and recognition, where strategies entwine,

A narrative of ambition and resilience, where excellence I'd refine.

Through the corporate hierarchy, where titles held sway,

I contemplated life's ascent in "Hierarchy's Way."

A journey through career progression, where goals align,

A story of aspirations and advancement, where success I'd define.

In the domain of innovation, where creativity thrived,

I delved into existence in "Innovation's Drive."

A quest for invention and transformation, where visions entwine,

A narrative of creativity and change, where progress I'd define.

In the world of investments, where fortunes were cast,

I ventured into "Investor's Vast."

A journey through financial strategies, where dreams align,

A tale of wealth and wisdom, where prosperity I'd define.

Onward I pressed, in the quest for life's essence,

Seeking clarity in business's language, in its presence.

In a world of numbers and strategies, where truths intertwine,

I explored the heart of existence, where purpose would shine.

Chapter 38

The Echoing Abyss of Meaning

The narrator's fear of meaninglessness

In TechnoExistence City, a surreal expanse so wide,
My journey took a darker, fearful ride.
Deep in its holographic heart, where data flowed like art,
I faced a paralyzing fear, a heavy, haunting part.

In a virtual auditorium, where avatars did debate,
Life's ROI and risks, our existence's cruel fate.
My fear loomed large, a ghostly, chilling sight,
A specter of meaninglessness, casting a shadow, blight.

"Why this obsolete code, in life's grand equation scheme,
Haunted by the void's specter, a never-ending dream?"
I quivered in uncertainty, as colleagues stood so tall,
Their lives charted and planned, on Gantt charts, they'd enthrall.

A neon sign above us, an emblem of our plight,
Swung between "Purpose" and "Void," in the auditorium's light.
In this bewildering realm, the fear grew like an algorithm,
Threatening to engulf us, a dark existential schism.

I questioned meaning in a world so set and sure,
As my words turned to binary, uncertain and obscure.
I pressed forward with courage, through this surreal domain,
To confront my fear of void, to find purpose once again.

In TechnoExistence City, where data streams would flow,
I faced the abyss, where meanings come and go.
In a world of success, I sought courage to decree,
That meaning could be found, even in the void, to be free.

In TechnoExistence City, where data streams would flow,
I confronted the abyss, where meanings ebb and go.
In the language of business, where jargon filled the air,
I pondered life's purpose, with a steadfast dare.

Amidst the stock market's frenzy, where values would sway,
I explored the depths of existence in "Price to Pay."
A journey through financial rollercoasters, where fortunes align,
A tale of wealth and self-discovery, where balance I'd define.

In the arena of competition, where rivals engaged in strife,
I navigated existence's challenges in "Competitive Life."
A quest for achievement and recognition, where strategies intertwine,
A narrative of resilience and perseverance, where success I'd redefine.

Through the corporate hierarchy, where titles held their might,
I contemplated life's journey in "Hierarchy's Height."
A journey through career's ups and downs, where aspirations align,
A story of growth and self-realization, where purpose I'd redesign.

In the realm of innovation, where creativity took its stance,
I delved into existence in "Innovation's Dance."
A quest for inspiration and transformation, where visions combine,
A narrative of adaptability and progress, where dreams I'd redefine.

In the world of investments, where choices would be vast,
I ventured into "Investor's Compass."
A journey through financial strategies, where goals intertwine,
A tale of prosperity and mindfulness, where fulfillment I'd define.

Onward I pressed, seeking life's true essence,
In the intricate web of business, with diligence and persistence.
In a world of numbers and plans, where challenges I'd embrace,
I discovered that meaning could thrive, even in the corporate space.

Chapter 39

The Quest in Quantum's Paradox

The narrator's exploration of different philosophies and religions

In the Quantum Metaverse's cryptic, neural maze,
I embarked on an odyssey, a profound craze.
Within a virtual agora, where philosophies took flight,
I sought life's true meaning amidst the neon data's light.

"Why the legacy code in this existential paradigm's might,
Navigating life's API, in search of purpose's sight?"
I questioned, observing colleagues' seamless parade,
Integrating belief systems in their life's grand charade.

A holographic sign swung, between "Faith" and "Certainty,"
Representing the ever-changing landscape of belief's certainty.
In this surreal realm, I journeyed far and wide,
Exploring belief currencies, in the digital divide.

Philosophical whitepapers and blockchain debates did ensue,
As I sought meaning, my purpose to construe.
My words became streams, philosophical and deep,
Contemplating life's essence, in a quest I'd keep.

Through the Quantum Metaverse, I ventured, brave and keen,
In search of existential truths, where meaning lay unseen.
In a world of purpose, I forged my unique trail,
In Quantum's paradox, I'd find meaning, without fail.

Through the Quantum Metaverse, I ventured, brave and keen,
In pursuit of existential truths, where meaning remained unseen.
Amidst the quantum entanglement, where dimensions converged,
In the language of business, my purpose emerged.

In the stock market's fluctuations, where values ebbed and flowed,
I delved into life's essence in "The Price We Owe."
A journey through financial complexity, where ethics intertwine,
A narrative of responsibility and conscience, where balance I'd define.

In the corporate competition, where strategies were deployed,
I contemplated life's journey in "The Game We Played."
A quest for recognition and success, where decisions align,
A story of ambition and self-awareness, where purpose I'd redesign.

Within the hierarchical structure, where titles held sway,
I explored existence in "The Roles We Play."
A journey through career's ups and downs, where aspirations aligned,
A tale of growth and self-discovery, where authenticity I'd find.

Innovation's realm beckoned, where creativity held might,
I immersed myself in "The Spark of Insight."
A quest for inspiration and change, where ideas combine,
A narrative of adaptability and progress, where dreams I'd redefine.

In the world of investments, where choices were vast,
I ventured through "The Investor's Forecast."
A journey through financial strategies, where goals intertwine,
A story of prosperity and mindfulness, where fulfillment I'd define.

With determination, I sought life's deepest layers,

In the quantum mysteries, where meaning was my prayers.

In a world of paradoxes, where uncertainty would hail,

I discovered that meaning thrived, even in the quantum's trail.

Chapter 40

The Quest for Digital Bonds

The narrator's search for connection with others

In Quantum's web, my surreal journey did commence,
A quest for connection, amidst the digital pretense.
Within the holographic marketplace, where synergy held sway,
Avatars sought connection, in a data-driven display.

"Why this legacy node in relational strategies, I implore,
Deciphering the neural paths, connection's secret core?"
I wondered, watching colleagues in their network ballet,
Their emotional KPIs signaling a successful relay.

A neon sign overhead, swinging between Connection and Isolation's call,
Symbolizing the enigma, my quest to conquer all.
In this bewildering realm, my quest took flight,
Navigating APIs and blockchain nodes, through the digital night.

A virtual odyssey, seeking connections genuine and true,
Bridging digital gaps, in a landscape all askew.
My words turned into streams, relational data's art,
Contemplating human bonds, from the core of the heart.

Through Quantum's metaverse, I journeyed without pause,
In search of real connection, breaking digital laws.
In a world of networks, I'd find the bonds I yearned,
For genuine human interaction, the quest I'd always discerned.

Through Quantum's metaverse, I journeyed without pause,

In pursuit of real connections, defying digital's constraints and laws.

Amidst the data streams, where algorithms churned,

In the language of business, I sought the lessons to be learned.

In the stock market's fluctuations, where values ebbed and flowed,

I ventured into life's essence in "The Price We Owe."

A quest for meaningful investments, where values would align,

A narrative of ethical choices, where purpose I'd redefine.

In the corporate competition, where strategies were employed,

I explored the essence of the game in "The Game We Played."

A journey through ambition's maze, where decisions intertwined,

A story of growth and self-discovery, where authenticity I'd find.

Within the organizational hierarchy, where titles held might,

I delved into existence in "The Roles We Play" at night.

A quest for identity and purpose, where roles would redesign,

A narrative of self-realization, where aspirations I'd realign.

In the realm of innovation, where creativity took flight,

I immersed myself in "The Spark of Insight" so bright.

A journey to inspire change and adaptation, where ideas would shine,

A tale of progress and adaptability, where dreams I'd redefine.

In the world of investments, where choices were vast,

I ventured through "The Investor's Forecast" so vast.

A journey through financial strategies, where goals I'd realign,

A story of prosperity and mindfulness, where fulfillment I'd define.

With determination, I delved into life's deepest layers,

In Quantum's enigmatic realm, where meaning was my prayers.

In a world of paradoxes, where uncertainty would prevail,

I discovered that genuine connection thrived, even in the quantum's trail.

Chapter 41

The Algorithm of Existence

The narrator's efforts to create meaning in his own life

Amidst the Quantum's ethereal threads, my journey carried on,
A quest for life's meaning, through a metaverse upon.
In a holographic agora, self-actualization's grand stage,
Avatars sought fulfillment, in a surreal digital age.

"Why this legacy code in my personalized quest?
Scripting existence's algorithm, seeking what's best?"
I pondered, while colleagues curated life's grand design,
Success metrics aligned with self-set KPIs so fine.

Above, a neon sign, flickered 'twixt Fulfillment and Ambiguity's call,
A mirror to my journey, my rise or my fall.
In this bewildering realm, I sought to create,
A life full of meaning, a personal, destined fate.

My quest became an odyssey, through self-help APIs I'd roam,
In the world of blockchain nodes, seeking a purpose and a home.
My words transformed to streams, of existential code and lore,
Unraveling life's mysteries, exploring its grand core.

In Quantum's metaverse, I ventured deep and wide,
Crafting my own existence, on this surreal data ride.
In a world of self-fulfillment, I'd find my own grace,
A meaningful life's algorithm, I'd finally embrace.

In Quantum's metaverse, I journeyed far and wide,
Navigating the data currents on this surreal digital tide.
In the language of business, I'd find my place,
Crafting a purposeful existence, in this vast cosmic space.

Through the stock market's fluctuations, where fortunes would
sway,
I sought my own wealth in "The Portfolio of Dreams" one day.
A quest for financial success, a path I'd carefully trace,
While balancing values and investments in this money-making
race.

Within the corporate corridors, where power was displayed,
I delved into "The Boardroom Paradox," where decisions were
weighed.
A journey through leadership's challenges, where ethics I'd base,
A narrative of influence and integrity, in this corporate embrace.

Amidst the organizational hierarchy, where titles held sway,
I explored my role in "The Power of Responsibility" at end of day.
A quest for impact and leadership, a path I'd gracefully pace,
While understanding that with power comes a greater duty to face.

In the realm of innovation, where creativity took flight,
I immersed myself in "The Genius of Disruption" so bright.
A journey to inspire change and adaptation, to leave a lasting trace,
A tale of innovation and transformation, in this visionary space.

In the world of investments, where choices were vast,

I ventured through "The Wealth of Well-Being" at last.

A journey through personal finance, where values I'd embrace,

A story of financial wisdom and holistic wealth, my own saving grace.

With determination, I embraced life's profound layers,

In Quantum's metaverse, where understanding was my prayers.

In a world of infinite possibilities, where meaning I'd chase,

I discovered that true fulfillment was found in life's embrace.

Chapter 42

The Code of Communion

The narrator's desire to find a sense of community

In the Digital Cosmos vast and wide, my journey did unfold,
A quest for heartfelt connections, a tale that's often told.
In a virtual realm of synergy, where data streams did flow,
I sought true camaraderie, in this surreal techno-show.

"Why am I this legacy protocol, in a world so interconnected?
Deciphering authentic bonds, where are they detected?"
I pondered, as colleagues thrived, in social harmony,
Belonging or isolation, my quest's dichotomy.

A neon sign above me swayed, between Isolation's shroud,
And Belonging's warm embrace, in a world so vast and loud.
In this mystic realm, my quest began, a digital odyssey,
Navigating social nodes and KPIs, seeking unity.

My journey transformed my words, into relational streams,
Exploring life's complexities, like travelers in their dreams.
In a world of digital bonds, I'd find the way,
To foster true connections, where hearts in unison sway.

In the boundless Digital Cosmos, my odyssey would unfurl,
In the search for human warmth, where kindred spirits swirl.
In a realm of data and code, I'd find what's real,
The code of communion, a treasure to reveal.

In the expansive Digital Cosmos, my odyssey did commence,
In pursuit of human connection, where data's mysteries dispense.
In a domain of algorithms, I yearned to understand,
The algorithm of empathy, a treasure within my hand.

Through the stock market's tumult, where fortunes rise and fall,
I navigated "The Portfolio of Human Bonds," a narrative to enthrall.
A quest for financial growth, in bonds of trust I'd invest,
Knowing that true riches lie in relationships, I was truly blessed.

Within the corporate arena, where competition fiercely thrived,
I explored "The Marketplace of Hearts," where success was derived.
A journey of leadership and compassion, I'd proudly face,
Realizing that in the business world, empathy held its own grace.

Amidst the technological whirlwind, where innovation did reign,
I delved into "The Symphony of Human Progress," a narrative plain.
A quest for advancement and social change, I'd strive to embrace,
Recognizing that in this digital age, humanity held its own place.

In the world of finance and stocks, where wealth could rapidly soar,
I ventured through "The Wealth of Empathetic Investing," wanting
more.
A journey to balance profit and purpose, in a financial space,
A story of socially responsible investing, a positive embrace.

With each step I took in the Digital Cosmos, my heart did swell,
In the search for genuine connections, where stories and experiences
dwell.
In a realm of technology and data, I discovered the real deal,
The power of empathy, a treasure so profound and surreal.

Chapter 43

The Code of Connection

The narrator's difficulty connecting with others

In the Digital Cosmos vast and grand,
A tale of connection in a data-driven land.
Within an amphitheater, where avatars convened,
My quest for bonds unseen.

"Why am I this legacy code," I mused and wondered,
In an ecosystem where connection's often squandered.
Interpersonal engagement, the algorithmic key,
To decipher in a world of complex esprit.

A neon sign, it swayed above, a paradox unfurled,
Between Engagement's vibrant dance and Disconnection's cold
whirl.
In this surreal realm, my odyssey did ignite,
Navigating APIs, emotional nodes, to find the light.

My journey spun my words into relational streams,
Exploring human intricacies, like seekers in their dreams.
In a world of data-driven links, I'd find my way,
To foster true connections, where hearts in unison sway.

In the sprawling Digital Cosmos, my odyssey would unfurl,
In the quest for human bonds, where souls together swirl.
In a realm of data and code, I'd find what's real,
The code of connection, a treasure to reveal.

In a digital realm where bytes abound,
My quest for connections, unbound.
Through the surreal technoscape, I'd dive,
Seeking bonds where data and hearts thrive.

Amidst the coding and software's domain,
I yearned for connections, not merely in vain,
For in this landscape of algorithms and code,
Lived the essence of bonds, in a complex ode.

Like a software engineer, I dared to explore,
The intricate dance of data, the human heart's core,
In pursuit of connections, both authentic and true,
In the world of technology, where data's value I knew.

With determination and wisdom, my journey unfurled,
Navigating this landscape, where networking's the world,
To bridge the divide between code and emotion's art,
And find the genuine bonds that reside in every heart.

Chapter 44

The Symphony of Connection

The narrator's hopes for finding connection

In the Digital Cosmos, a tale I entwine,
Of connection and hope, in a world so divine.
Within a holographic arena, I dreamt and I yearned,
For authentic connections, where hearts brightly burned.

"Why am I this legacy code," I pondered so deep,
In a matrix of algorithms, where connections did creep.
A roadmap to follow, with aspirations so grand,
To weave the tapestry of bonds, across this vast land.

A neon sign flickered, its message so bright,
Between "Connection" and "Potential," in the vast sea of light.
In this surreal world, my hopes took their flight,
Navigating the nodes, with all of my might.

My journey transformed words into data streams,
Filled with optimism, with dreams and grand schemes.
In this sprawling metaverse, with hopes so true,
I'd kindle connections, both old and brand new.

In the Digital Cosmos, I forged my own way,
To create lasting bonds that would forever stay.
In a world of technology, where data did gleam,
I wove the symphony of connection, a beautiful dream.

In the vast Digital Cosmos, I charted my course,
In search of connections, a powerful force.
In this realm of technology, where algorithms reign,
I set out to prove that true bonds could sustain.

Much like a software engineer, I crafted with care,
Lines of connection in the digital air,
For in the world of data, where everything's in sight,
I aimed to show that genuine bonds held might.

With each line of code, I built bridges of trust,
Practical wisdom guiding, as bonds were robust,
In the Digital Cosmos, where data's the stream,
I proved that connections could be more than a dream.

Chapter 45

The Echoes of Mortality

The narrator's thoughts about his own death

In the Virtual Eternity Matrix vast,
A surreal journey began, an existential cast.
In an amphitheater of life's grand design,
I pondered death, a task quite divine.

"Why am I this legacy frame," I mused in my chair,
Amidst mortality metrics, a weight hard to bear.
Existence's return, in this realm did I seek,
Balancing life's ledger, with data unique.

A neon sign above, in hues it did sway,
Between "Legacy" and "Transcendence," its nightly display.
In this bewildering world, thoughts of death took their flight,
Navigating blockchain nodes, in the realm of the finite.

A virtual odyssey, this journey profound,
Through calculations of mortality, on data I'd bound.
In a world of immortality, where life's light did gleam,
I embraced the echoes of mortality, a profound human dream.

My words turned to data, in the matrix's song,
Weighing life's purpose, where I truly belong.
In this surreal metaverse, I sought to find grace,
In the dance of mortality, in life's fleeting embrace.

Through the technoscape I ventured, so brave and so bold,
To understand the limits of mortality's hold.
In a world of optimization, where data did blend,
I sought to grasp life's essence, from beginning to end.

Through the technoscape I ventured, with algorithms in hand,
Seeking the secrets of life, in this surreal data land.
In a world of optimization, where metrics run high,
I explored mortality's boundaries, reaching for the sky.

Much like a data analyst, I analyzed each thread,
Seeking patterns in existence, where answers might be spread.
For in the world of data, where numbers often deceive,
I aimed to find the wisdom, the knowledge I'd achieve.

With each data point studied, and each insight I'd glean,
Practical wisdom guided me, like a guiding beam,
Through the technoscape I journeyed, my quest unending,
In search of life's meaning, in this data-driven blending.

Chapter 46

The Conundrum of the Uncharted

The narrator's fear of the unknown

In the Quantum Metaverse vast and surreal,
My quest, a profound ordeal.
An odyssey in the digital domain,
To conquer fear and its relentless reign.

In a holographic citadel, uncertainty's lair,
Where simulations danced in the digital air.
Avatars assessed, in data's embrace,
The ROI of venturing into the unknown space.

"Why am I the legacy code," I mused,
As in uncertainty's fortress, my thoughts were infused.
Navigating binary precipices, both high and low,
In this realm where the unknown's tendrils did grow.

Above the citadel, neon signs in sway,
Between "Exploration" and "Caution" held their display.
Symbolic of the paradox, fear intertwined,
In this landscape where digital frontiers I'd find.

A journey of virtual odyssey's grace,
Through uncharted blockchains, in this bewildering place.
To decode the enigma, where data held sway,
O'er the human fear of the unknown, each day.

My words turned to streams, analytical, profound,
Bearing the weight of fear, on this journey unbound.
In the metaverse's tapestry, intricate and vast,
I sought to unveil the unknown at last.

I pressed ever onward, with courage and might,
To face the abyss, in the digital night.
In a landscape of risk, and data's embrace,
I danced with the unknown, in this surreal space.

In data's embrace, I set my sight,
To navigate the digital night.
In landscapes where risk and data race,
I danced with courage, embraced the chase.

Algorithms wove a complex theme,
In this surreal, digital dream.
With terms like "AI" and "machine's glance,
" I learned to lead the code's advance.

Adapting to the ever-changing scene,
Agile steps and methods keen.
For in this world of endless height,
Flexibility is my guiding light.

As I journeyed to the digital's core,
A horizon unknown, I'd explore.
Innovation's pulse, the heart's delight,
Guided me through the endless night.

Chapter 47

The Algorithm of Torment

The narrator's fear of pain and suffering

In the Cybernetic Cosmos, surreal and vast,
My journey took flight, through shadows it cast.
Into my psyche's depths, I would descend,
 Fear of pain and suffering, my constant friend.

Within neural arenas, holographic and grand,
Where avatars analyzed thoughts, on demand.
Cognitive entropy, suffering's cost to calculate,
In the language of ICT, I faced my fate.

"Why am I the legacy, in this cerebral space,
Calculating the matrix, in this intricate place?"
I pondered aloud, as colleagues, data-wise,
Mastered pain, through digital stoic eyes.

Above the arena, neon signs would sway,
Between "Endurance" and "Reduction," each day.
A symbol of torment's paradoxical creed,
In a world where suffering, I sought to impede.

A surreal odyssey, my fear took its flight,
Through virtual receptors, in the vastness of night.
Navigating through algorithms, seeking to decode,
The essence of agony, in this digital abode.

As I journeyed, my words turned to code,

Bearing the weight of the fear, in this labyrinth I rode.

In the Cybernetic Cosmos, so vast and complex,

I sought to confront suffering, with courage and reflex.

I pressed on, determined, 'midst data and strife,

To face the abyss, in the digital life.

In this realm of pain management, my goal was concise,

To understand torment, and the human soul's price.

With resolve, I journeyed, through data's vast sea,

Exploring the depths where pain's shadows could be.

In this realm of suffering, I sought a new way,

To ease the burdens carried through night and through day.

With "analytics" and "trend analysis" as my guide,

I ventured to comfort, side by side.

For in the realm of pain, where afflictions are rife,

I aimed to bring solace and relieve inner strife.

With empathy and data, I wove a fine thread,

Understanding that healing means more than just meds.

In this journey surreal, where pain's web did entwine,

I aspired to bring comfort, in this digital time.

Chapter 48

The Algorithm of Denial

The narrator's denial of his own mortality

In the Quantum Data Abyss, vast and surreal,
My journey took flight, my fears to unseal.
Deep in existential chasm, I ventured to cope,
With my fear of death, through the ICT's professional scope.

Within the holographic interface's unique plane,
Existential avoidance, a complex domain.
Avatars executed algorithms, a cerebral strife,
Against impending entropy, to evade the end of life.

"Why am I the deprecated code," I mused in thought,
In this fortress of death avoidance, where answers sought.
Executing subroutines to hide life's decay,
As colleagues built denial matrices, to keep it all at bay.

Above the interface, neon signs would sway,
Between "Evasion" and "Acceptance," the internal fray.
A symbol of the battle, my mind did wage,
In a world where impermanence, I wished to disengage.

A surreal odyssey, denial's path I'd tread,
Through cognitive encryption nodes, where secrets spread.
To decrypt mortality's enigma, in this virtual domain,
Where digital immortality often obscured the human bane.

My words transformed to intricate code, so deep,
Bearing the weight of denial, in this journey, I'd keep.
In the Quantum Data Abyss, I sought to understand,
The truth of mortality, amidst the digital land.

I pressed forward, resolute, through this virtual fight,
To confront the void, with courage and insight.
In a world of digital defense, where many would roam,
I embraced the human essence, and found my way home.

With determination, I journeyed, through the digital night,
To face the unknown, with heart full of light.
In a realm of cybersecurity, where threats often loom,
I defended with purpose, dispelling the gloom.

With firewalls and encryption, I guarded the gate,
Understanding that data's the world's modern fate.
In this landscape surreal, where cyber-dangers did swarm,
I shielded the digital realm, protecting from harm.

With courage and insight, I stood as the guard,
In this world where cybersecurity wasn't taken too hard.
In this virtual fight, where data's the gold,
I protected the treasures, ensuring stories were told.

Chapter 49

The Quantum Solace Equation

The narrator's search for comfort and reassurance

In the Quantum Molecular Nexus, a world entwined,
My surreal journey began, a quest defined.
Seeking comfort and reassurance, I'd embark,
In ICT's abstract language, where data's spark.

Within the reactor of existential solace's glow,
Avatars executed algorithms, a celestial flow.
Engaged in quantum encryption, a surreal dance,
My quest for solace, a delicate chance.

"Why am I the deprecated molecule," I sighed,
In a quantum solution, elusive fragments to provide.
Bonding with reassurance, like atoms in the dance,
My colleagues, entangling bonds, took a quantum stance.

Above the reactor, neon signs would sway,
Between "Reassurance" and "Uncertainty," night and day.
A symbol of the balance, my heart did seek,
In a world where digital odds often made me weak.

A surreal odyssey, through quantum probability's grace,
Navigating through emotional resonance, a delicate space.
Seeking the chemistry of solace, in this digital domain,
Where human emotions battled data's reign.

My words transformed, equations intricate and true,
Bearing the weight of longing, a human cue.
For reassurance, solace, I'd journey through,
In the Quantum Molecular Nexus, where hearts anew.

I pressed forward, resolute, in my digital stride,
To find emotional bonds, where solace did reside.
In a world of quantum probabilities, where data would roam,
I embraced the human essence, and found comfort's home.

In the vast quantum realm, I ventured with grace,
To explore the connections that time couldn't erase.
In a landscape of qubits, where reality took flight,
I sought emotional bonds, amidst the data's light.

With entanglement's dance, I wove a new thread,
In this quantum probability where stories were spread.
In this digital voyage, where paths intertwined,
I discovered a haven where solace I'd find.

In the tapestry of data, I found my own tune,
Embracing the human essence, under the digital moon.
In this boundless quantum, where possibilities bloom,
I uncovered connections, dispelling the gloom.

Chapter 50

The Quantum Alchemy of Purpose

The narrator's efforts to find meaning in life

I journey through the Quantum Molecular Nexus,
A world in flux, an existential crux.
Seeking life's true meaning, in ICT's dance I sway,
In a realm where quantum secrets held the day.

Within the holographic lab of existential grace,
Avatars analyze quantum realms, a mystic chase.
Engaged in entropy's reduction, a dance so bright,
My quest for meaning, a profound light.

"Why am I the legacy element?" I confide,
In this quantum equation, life's purpose to decide.
Catalyzing the compound of existence, I aspire,
As colleagues manipulate molecules in a dance of fire.

Above the lab, neon signs waver and gleam,
"Purpose" and "Ambiguity," like an elusive dream.
Symbolic of the quest my heart does seek,
In a world of digital odds, where answers felt meek.

A surreal odyssey through quantum states I tread,
Navigating through the labyrinth, where meaning's spread.
Deciphering life's chemistry, amidst quantum entwined,
In a world where data reigned, I sought what's undefined.

My words transform, into equations complex and grand,
Bearing the weight of my quest, across the land.
For meaning, for purpose, I'd journey through,
In the Quantum Molecular Nexus, where skies are blue.

Pressing onward, resolute, in this enigmatic space,
To uncover life's essence, in this vast embrace.
In a world of quantum probabilities, where data did roam,
I embraced the human spirit and found purpose's home.

I journey forth, resolute, in the quantum expanse,
To decipher life's riddles in this intricate dance.
In a realm of probabilities, where data streams flow,
I embrace the human spirit, let its brilliance show.

In the quantum symphony, where particles entwine,
I seek the essence of life, in the data's design.
In this digital world, where mysteries would unfurl,
I find purpose and meaning, a precious pearl.

Through quantum uncertainty, I follow the trace,
To grasp life's true essence, in this boundless space.
In a world of data's probabilities and infinite chrome,
I cherish humanity and find my true home.

Chapter 51

The Synaptic Quest for Serenity

The narrator's turn to religion or spirituality

I journey through the Synaptic Health Matrix, vast and deep,
A promise to keep, a quest to keep.
For comfort profound, serene and sure,
In a fusion of worlds, my quest will endure.

Within the holographic symposium's grand sight,
Where avatars ponder through the day and night.
Neural entropy and resilience's grace,
My search for comfort will find its place.

"Why am I the quiescent neuron?"
I sigh, In a synaptic strategy session, I confide.
Exploring the nexus of assurance and more,
Religion and spirituality I'd explore.

Colleagues perform psychological deeds,
Optimizing my emotions, addressing my needs.
Emotional portfolios, intelligence metrics told,
Awareness of spiritual solace, a story to unfold.

Above, neon signs dance and sway,
Between "Faith" and "Resilience," I'd convey.
A dual nature of my quest, complex and grand,
In a world of medical data, I'd make my stand.

A surreal odyssey, through devotion I roam,
Corridors of spirituality, pathways to roam.
Seeking the chemistry, where souls would unite,
In a world of data, I'd seek spiritual light.

My words transform, into neurochemical art,
A quest for comfort, a journey from the heart.
In the synaptic realm, a fusion so pure,
I'd find solace and serenity, that's for sure.

Pressing onward, resolute, I'd explore,
The essence of comfort, I'd yearn for more.
In a mental landscape, complex and so vast,
I'd find spiritual sanctuary, at last.

I venture forth, with spirit full of zest,
In search of comfort's essence, to put my soul at rest.
Through neurons' intricate pathways, I'd boldly roam,
Exploring the mental landscape, seeking a sacred home.

In the cerebral expanse, where thoughts did intertwine,
I journey through synapses, in a grand design.
In the realm of consciousness, where neurons held their sway,
I seek spiritual sanctuary, where tranquility lay.

With each cognitive voyage, in the labyrinth of my mind,
I yearn to find the solace I've strived to unwind.
In the tapestry of thoughts, where ideas amassed,
I discover spiritual sanctuary, at long last.

Chapter 52

The Neurocorporate Quest for Love

The narrator's search for love and support

I journey through the Neurocorporate Nexus, vast and profound,
On a quest for love, my heart unbound.
Amid synapses intricate, my path is clear,
A quest for love and support, no room for fear.

Within the holographic conference's grand design,
Affective investments, emotions so fine.
ROI of bonds and emotional wealth,
My quest for love, a pursuit of stealth.

"Why am I the dormant receptor?" I say,
In this summit of feelings, I'll find my way.
Exploring the portfolio, love's tender grace,
In a world of business precision, a unique embrace.

Colleagues diversify, emotional ties we mend,
Relational metrics, an approach to amend.
Equity in connections, both astute and bold,
In a dualistic world, where warmth and isolation unfold.

On a virtual odyssey, through emotions I stride,
Hedging strategies, algorithms to confide.
Decoding the anatomy of love, so intricate and divine,
In a world of data, where emotions entwine.

My words transform into emotional equations,
A quest for love, amidst complex relations.
In the surreal emotional realm I dwell,
Seeking the core of the human tale to tell.

Pressing forward, resolute, I'll explore,
The essence of love, in my heart's deep core.
In an emotional landscape, a complex grand view,
I'll find connection, love, and support too.

With purpose aflame, I press ahead,
In search of love's true essence, to claim its sacred thread.
Through the labyrinth of emotions, intricate and vast,
I seek connection's sanctuary, where love could forever last.

In the realm of feelings, where heartstrings gently strum,
I journey through the landscapes, where emotions become one.
In the tapestry of affections, where compassion holds its sway,
I discover connection's sanctuary, where love forever lay.

With each heartfelt encounter, in the intricate web of emotions,
I yearn to find the essence of love's endless devotions.
In the embrace of understanding, where empathy surpasses,
I uncover connection's sanctuary, a love that eternally amasses.

Chapter 53

The Quest for Vital Fulfillment

The narrator's attempts to make the most of his life

In the Neurocorporate Nexus, vast and grand,
I embark on a journey, to seek life's command.
Amidst the holographic symposium, I dwell,
Optimizing existence, a story to tell.

"Why am I the dormant mitochondrion?" I plea,
In this metabolic assembly, a journey to see.
Exploring the pathways, existence's rhyme,
In a world of data, I bide my time.

Colleagues fine-tuned, our life dashboards on display,
Health optimization, a systematic way.
Metrics reflected in this intricate scheme,
A dance between data and life's vibrant dream.

A virtual odyssey through databases vast,
Well-being ROI, calculations amassed.
Decoding physiology, life's grand scheme,
In a world of healthcare, I live my dream.

My words transformed into biological equations,
A quest for life's essence, amidst aspirations.
In a surreal health-focused realm I embark,
Seeking the core of life, amidst the data's spark.

Pressing forward, resolute, I'll explore,

The essence of life, to the very core.

In a wellness landscape, intricate and bright,

I'll seize every moment, in the quest for light.

I ventured forth with purpose, my spirit set ablaze,

To grasp the essence of life's most brilliant rays.

In the realm of well-being, where vitality took flight,

I embraced each precious moment, seeking radiant light.

Through the labyrinth of wellness, my journey to unfold,

I sought the secrets of life, a story to be told.

In the tapestry of health, where vitality did ignite,

I seized every opportunity, in my quest for boundless light.

With each step I took, in the landscape of the living,

I yearned to find the essence of a life so forgiving.

In the embrace of vitality, where wellness shone so bright,

I discovered life's sanctuary, a radiant, eternal sight.

Chapter 54

Dreams in the Nexus: A Journey of Self-Realization

The narrator's hopes for himself

In the Neurocorporate Nexus, where networks embrace,
I dance with my dreams, in a timeless space.
Amidst the symposium, where hopes take their stand,
I weave my dreams, with a skillful hand.

"Why am I the dormant neuron?" I muse,
In this cognitive summit, where dreams infuse.
Navigating pathways, of aspirations' gleam,
In a world of data, where dreams are supreme.

Colleagues meticulously, craft life's grand design,
Strategic ambition, a brilliant intertwine.
Ambition indices, in this complex theme,
A dance between data and a future's beam.

A virtual odyssey, through algorithms I roam,
Future-potential ROI, where dreams find a home.
Deciphering the anatomy of my soul's desire,
In a world where data might quench the fire.

Words transformed into cognitive equations,
A quest for my dreams, amidst life's foundations.
In this surreal landscape, ambition takes flight,
In the quest for a future, bathed in radiant light.

Pressing onward, determined, I strive,

To unlock my hopes, and truly come alive.

In a world of planning, where dreams unfurl,

I'll discover my essence, the heart of my world.

I pressed forward with resolve, on a mission so bold,

To unlock the treasures of dreams, in a landscape untold.

In a realm of strategic planning, where visions did swirl,

I uncovered my essence, the heart of life's pearl.

Through the labyrinth of aspirations, I ventured to roam,

In search of the essence of dreams, in this mystical dome.

In the canvas of ambition, where possibilities did twirl,

I unearthed my purpose, the heart of the world.

With each step I took, in the journey of ambition,

I yearned to find the essence of life's grand mission.

In the realm of aspirations, where dreams did swirl,

I discovered my legacy, the heart of the world.

Chapter 55

Society's Symphony: A Journey of Shared Aspiration

The narrator's hopes for others

In the Neurocorporate Nexus, a vast neural domain,
I embark on a journey, compassion my main aim.
Amidst the symposium on collective well-being,
Hope for others in my heart's careening.

"Why am I the dormant synapse?" I ponder,
In a sociological assembly, aspirations yonder.
Navigating pathways of goodwill and grace,
In this data-driven world, a compassionate place.

Colleagues meticulously calibrate their dashboards,
Social impact measured, hope's embers ablaze.
Compassion indices in a systematic theme,
In a world where data often steals the dream.

A virtual odyssey through altruism's domain,
Social welfare algorithms, a compassionate gain.
Deciphering the sociology of communal upliftment,
In a world where medical data's the dominant sentiment.

Words transformed into sociological rhyme,
A quest for hope, amidst the complex paradigm.
In this surreal landscape, dreams found their hold,
For a better society, a story to be told.

Pressing onward, I'll tirelessly strive,
To unlock my hopes, helping others thrive.
In a world of optimization, where data took the curl,
I'll discover the essence of hope for the world.

I pressed onward with unwavering drive,
Unlocking possibilities, helping others thrive.
In a realm of optimization, where data did swirl,
I discovered the essence of hope for the world.

Through the landscape of efficiency, I'd explore,
Finding ways to make life's blessings pour.
In a world of analytics, where insights did unfurl,
I unearthed the essence of hope for the world.

With each effort I made, in my quest for good,
I aimed to uplift others, as I knew I should.
In the realm of progress, where potential did twirl,
I embraced the essence of hope for the world.

Chapter 56

Harmony's Reverie: A Global Quest for Hope

The narrator's hopes for the world

In the Neurocorporate Nexus, where networks entwined,
My quest for global hope, my vision unconfined.
Surreal summits unfurled, global voices arose,
To map out a future, where hope finds repose.

With societal impact and ROI's keen sight,
My dreams took their flight, bathed in radiant light.

"Why am I the dormant receptor?" I ponder and muse,
Navigating the labyrinth, hope I shall choose.
In the global strategy, a bright future I see,
In the world's transformation, where we must be.

Colleagues observed with meticulous care,
Fine-tuned dashboards, a world to repair.
Sustainability indices, a systematic embrace,
To make our world better, hope's guiding grace.

A virtual odyssey through models we'd weave,
Ecological equilibrium, the world to relieve.
Deciphering global harmony, with data to unfurl,
In a world where medical data often took the swirl.

Words transformed into planetary rhyme,
A quest for hope, a sign of the time.
In this surreal landscape, dreams took their hold,
For a better world, a story to be told.

Pressing onward, I tirelessly strove,
Unlocking my hopes, with compassion I rove.
In a world of optimization, where data's the pearl,
I'll find the essence of hope for the world.

Pressing onward, I tirelessly strive,
Unlocking my hopes, with compassion I thrive.
In a world of optimization, where data's the pearl,
I'll find the essence of hope for the world.

In the realm of metrics, where numbers take flight,
I'll seek paths to make the world truly bright.
With efficiency's compass and progress to unfurl,
I'll uncover the essence of hope for the world.

My journey continues with purpose in sight,
To make a difference and bring forth the light.
In the landscape of analytics, where insights would swirl,
I'll embody the essence of hope for the world.

Chapter 57

The Quantum Equation of Compassion

The narrator's actions to help others

In the Quantum Calculus Nexus, a realm vast and grand,
My journey continued, with purpose close at hand.
To make a difference, my fervent quest,
Amidst modern math's complexities, I'd be the best.

In a holographic symposium, quantum and surreal,
I gathered with avatars, a sense of purpose I'd unveil.
Nonlinear optimizations, benevolence's grand prize,
In the quantum world, compassion would rise.

"Why am I the dormant eigenvalue?" I'd question and ponder,
Navigating through equations, the mathematical wonder.
Altruistic intervention, coordinates intricate and wise,
In the realm of compassion, I'd make the world's skies.

My colleagues manipulated quantum philanthropy, precise,
With indices charitable, we rolled the dice.
Transformation and stasis, a neon sign's dance,
In the quantum realm, where compassion found its chance.

Our actions became an odyssey, virtual and bold,
Through equations and entanglement, compassion we'd unfold.
Mathematical abstractions, our guide and our curse,
Yet we'd focus on betterment, not the equations' terse verse.

Our words transformed into equations, a language profound,
The weight of our efforts, in each math piece was found.
To make a difference, to society's heart, we'd profess,
Amidst equations and progress, we'd bring forth success.

In this mathematics-focused land surreal,
We'd unlock the essence, with compassion as our keel.
In a world of optimization, equations, our prism,
We'd make a difference, a mathematical altruism.

In this surreal land of mathematics, I'll unlock the essence,
with compassion as my compass.
In a world of optimization, equations my guide,
I'll make a difference, with mathematical altruism by my side.

Through algorithms and numbers, I'll deftly chart,
A course of change, a compassionate heart.
In this landscape of data, where patterns unfurl,
I'll embody the essence of hope for the world.

My journey continues with formulas in play,
To illuminate the path and light up the day.
In the realm of mathematics, where precision does twirl,
I'll embody the essence of hope for the world.

Chapter 58

The Quantum Symphony of Dedication

The narrator's commitment to making the world a better place

In the Quantum Calculus Nexus, where abstraction reigned
supreme,
My surreal journey unfolded, like an elusive dream.
A commitment unwavering, I was here to embrace,
In the world of mathematics, in this complex space.

Amidst holographic symposiums, where equations took flight,
Multidimensional avatars, united in our might.
Tensorial impacts, global change's immense grace,
My dedication at the symposium's embrace.

"Why am I the latent eigenvector?" I'd ponder and peer,
Navigating dimensions, bringing change near and clear.
Altruistic calculus, an intricate dance so grand,
In the pursuit of betterment, I'd take a bold stand.

Colleagues fine-tuned transformation, tensors so deft,
Metrics of optimization, the symposium's quest.
Progress and stagnation, a neon sign's grace,
In this quantum realm, where dedication had its place.

My commitment was an odyssey, a virtual flight,
Through mathematical equations, I'd bring forth the light.
Intricate geometry, societal change's advance,
In a world of abstraction, I'd give it a chance.

My words became expressions, mathematics profound,
The weight of my commitment, in each equation was found.
To make the world better, I'd digress,
Amidst formulas and progress, I'd truly impress.

In this mathematical land surreal,
I'd unlock the essence, with a dedication so real.
In a world of optimization, formulas and impress,
I'd make the world better, a mathematical success.

In this surreal land of mathematics, I'll unlock the essence,
with dedication as my compass.
In a world of optimization, formulas my guide,
I'll make the world better, with mathematical success by my side.

With algorithms and numbers, I'll deftly engineer,
Solutions to problems, both far and near.
In this realm of mathematics, where equations coalesce,
I'll epitomize the essence of hope, I confess.

My journey persists, with calculations in flight,
To brighten the future, with mathematical might.
In this world of numbers, where patterns progress,
I'll embody the essence of hope, no less.

Chapter 59

The Fractal Dreams of Change

The narrator's belief that change is possible

In the Quantum Calculus Nexus, colors intertwined,
A kaleidoscope realm where realities entwined.
My journey, surreal and vast,
With profound belief, my die was cast.

Amidst a holographic symposium's embrace,
Where mathematical wonders took their place.
Probabilistic transformations in the quantum tide,
Fractal potentials, where my dreams could ride.

"Why am I the latent fractal dimension?" I mused,
Navigating probabilities, my faith not confused.
Metamorphosis in equations, a path I'd choose,
In the Nexus's heart, where hope would amuse.

Colleagues, avatars, in a probabilistic trance,
Adjusting change matrices, in a cosmic dance.
Transformational indices, systematic and bold,
The neon sign's flicker, in stories yet untold.

"Adaptation" and "Inertia," symbols of the day,
In a surreal landscape where belief held sway.
My odyssey virtual, through probabilities vast,
A quest for change, in equations so steadfast.

Words turned to equations, probabilistic in grace,
The weight of belief in every embrace.
The potential for change, I'd dare to profess,
In uncertainties' midst, my dreams would impress.

In the Quantum Calculus Nexus, a narrative so strange,
The fractal dreams of change, destined to rearrange.
A journey surreal, where probabilities dance,
In the quest for transformation, my hopes did enhance.

In the Quantum Calculus Nexus, a narrative so strange,
Where relativity's embrace, created a cosmic change.
A journey surreal, where spacetime did expand,
In the quest for transformation, I'd take my stand.

With Einstein's theories guiding my way,
I ventured through realms where realities sway.
In this world of relativistic dreams, a quantum trance,
I'd decipher the essence of change's cosmic dance.

As I traversed dimensions, through time's endless flow,
I'd unlock secrets, where quantum possibilities grow.
In the Quantum Calculus Nexus, where I'd advance,
I'd grasp the essence of change, in this cosmic expanse.

Chapter 60

The Fractal Symphony of Change

The narrator's belief in the importance of action

In the Quantum Calculus Nexus, a kaleidoscope's domain,
My journey surreal, far from mundane.
My belief in change, profound and bright,
In the complexities of math, I'd find my light.

Amidst a holographic symposium's artful dance,
Probabilistic functions in a cosmic trance.
Stochastic convergence, fractal dreams anew,
Change vectors evaluated, a vision so true.

"Why am I the latent fractal dimension?" I cried,
Through transformative equations, my hopes implied.
Navigating intricate probabilities, I took a chance,
In the Nexus's heart, where change would enhance.

Colleagues adjusted matrices with stochastic grace,
Transformational indices in this cosmic space.
The neon sign swayed, an enigmatic sign,
"Adaptation" and "Inertia," a dance so divine.

My odyssey surreal, through probabilities vast,
In pursuit of change, my hopes steadfast.
Words transformed to equations, in patterns I'd glean,
Belief in transformation, the essence of my dream.

In this Quantum Calculus Nexus, surreal and strange,
A symphony of change, destined to rearrange.
In mathematical mazes, my belief did bloom,
In the dance of uncertainties, I'd find my room.

Through fractal dimensions, I'd chart my own course,
In the quest for transformation, a cosmic force.
A journey in math, where uncertainties swirl,
My belief in change, a transcendent pearl.

Through fractal dimensions, I'll boldly explore,
In the realm of relative theories, I'll seek to implore.
A journey through spacetime, where concepts will twirl,
My faith in transformation, like a radiant pearl.

With relativistic wisdom as my guiding star,
I'll navigate the cosmos, both near and far.
In this mathematical voyage, where equations will swirl,
I'll uncover the essence of change, in a cosmic whirl.

As I delve into relativity's embrace,
I'll decipher the secrets of time and space.
Through fractal dimensions, where possibilities unfurl,
I'll grasp the true meaning of change, in this cosmic whirl.

Chapter 61

The Sacred Labyrinth of Surrender

The narrator's willingness to sacrifice for his beliefs

Amidst the ethereal tapestries where mysteries unwind,
The Divine Labyrinth's path, where faith entwined.
My journey, surreal, profound, and deep,
In ancient religious terms, my promises to keep.

In celestial contemplation, a sanctuary grand,
Where seraphic beings, devoutly take their stand.
Architects of sacrifice, they pondered, wondered why,
My path through faith, a sacred sky.

"Why am I the penitent, in this hallowed space,
Navigating labyrinthine rites, seeking sacred grace?"
My thoughts in whispers, the journey to embark,
In devotion's embrace, I'd find the sacred spark.

Celestial beings, in transcendence I believed,
Sacrifices performed, in faith I'd achieved.
A sigil radiant, a symbol strong and bright,
"Devotion" and "Revelation," a dance of cosmic light.

My sacrifice, a celestial odyssey told,
Through esoteric prayers, my faith would unfold.
In sacred geometry, my devotion would abide,
In a realm where symbols in the heart would reside.

In the ethereal metaverse, my words did take flight,
Celestial hymns, a beacon of divine light.
A devotion so pure, a connection I'd find,
In the sacred dance of faith, heart, and mind.

Through this faith-focused land, I'd boldly tread,
Unlocking the essence of surrender, where faith led.
I sacred rituals' tongue, my tale would weave,
A journey of surrender, in the quest to believe.

In the realm of faith, I'd firmly stride,
Where sacred teachings would be my guide.
In spiritual verses, my story would interweave,
A journey of surrender, where faith would relieve.

With Spirit's wisdom, I'd seek the divine,
In the land of devotion, where hearts would incline.
Through sacred scriptures, my spirit would cleave,
A journey of surrender, in the quest to believe.

With faith as my compass, I'd venture and roam,
In Spirit's embrace, I'd find my true home.
In the language of devotion, my soul would perceive,
A journey of surrender, where faith would never leave.

In the sanctuary of belief, I'd find my reprieve,
In the presence of Spirit, I'd courageously cleave.
Through chapters of devotion, my faith would achieve,
A journey of surrender, where faith would eternally relieve.

Chapter 62

The Celestial Symphony of Hope

The narrator's hope that his actions will make a difference

Amidst tapestries resplendent, where the divine's embrace,
My journey unfolds, in this celestial place.
Rich in ancient terms, my path deeply entwined,
With hope to make a difference, a transcendent bind.

In the sanctuary's grace, where seraphic voices sing,
Invoking ancient liturgies, on celestial wing.
Divine calculations, I ponder, I soar,
My aspirations in the cosmic chord.

"Why am I, the humble one, in this sacred land,
Navigating labyrinthine faith, by celestial hand?"
My voice, a whisper, amidst devotion's grace,
Seeking cosmic reverberations, a celestial trace.

Celestial beings, in benevolence,
I believe, Rites of cosmic kindness,
my heart I conceive. A radiant sigil, above, pulsing strong and bright,
"Intervention" and "Mystery," in the celestial light.

My aspiration, a celestial odyssey foretold,
Through sacred hymns, my hopes would unfold.
In the intricate geometry of cosmic influence's plan,
In a realm where symbolism met the dreams of man.

In the ethereal metaverse, my words took flight,
Celestial verses, aglow with guiding light.
Hope carried on the breeze, as I reached for the skies,
To shape the cosmos, where my aspirations lie.

Through this faith-focused land, I'd find my way,
Unlocking the essence of hope, come what may.
In a realm of sacred agency, my tale I'd share,
Believing in my actions, to shape the cosmic air.

In a journey inspired by faith's grand scheme,
I'd traverse the circles, like a vivid dream.
In realms of devotion, where devotion's fires flare,
Believing in my mission, to purify the spiritual air.

With divine guidance, I'd walk the path,
Through circles of salvation, escaping sin's wrath.
In sacred landscapes, my soul I'd prepare,
Believing in redemption, to purify the spiritual air.

In the verses of devotion, I'd find the light,
Through celestial realms, a spiritual flight.
In the language of the heart, my soul laid bare,
Believing in heavenly ascent, to purify the spiritual air.

With faith as my poet, I'd ascend the spheres,
To reach the Empyrean, casting off earthly fears.
In verses and prayers, my soul I'd declare,
Believing in transcendence, to purify the spiritual air.

Chapter 63

Labyrinth of the Psyche: A Surreal Odyssey

The narrator's inability to remember where he is or why he is there

Amidst labyrinthine corridors, in this peculiar domain,
My journey unfolds, in the Psychedelic Asylum's reign.
My mind, a kaleidoscope, with uncertainty adorned,
Complex psychiatric terms, my psyche was adorned.

Reality and illusion, in this realm, intertwined,
I grappled with what I'd find.
Lost within myself, purpose far from sight,
In the asylum's labyrinth, I searched for the light.

"Why am I, the lost fragment, in my own cognition's haze,
Adrift in corridors of thought, lost in a mental maze?"
My confusion profound, like a riddle left unsaid,
A flickering neon sign above, "Lucidity" and "Chaos" it read.

In this surreal dimension, disorientation took its toll,
A hallucinatory odyssey, a puzzle for the soul.
Twisted alleys of consciousness, memories entwined,
Psychology's intricate dance, in the depths of my mind.

Through this mental metaverse, thoughts like colors swirled,
Kaleidoscopic patterns, in this strange mental world.
In the sea of my thoughts, turbulent and grand,
I sought an anchor, in this unfamiliar land.

I pressed forward, determined, in this psyche's grace,
To unearth my disorientation, to find a clearer place.
In a realm of mental health, where words often get lost,
Grappling with my own shadows, no matter the cost.

In the labyrinth of my subconscious mind,
I delve to understand my thoughts, where mysteries bind.
In the realm of dreams, where symbols dance and swirl,
I confront my inner demons, my heart's unfurled.

Through the tangled web of my psyche's design,
I navigate the corridors, where memories entwine.
In the domain of introspection, where fears reside,
I face my deepest shadows, with courage as my guide.

In the depths of my subconscious, a labyrinthine place,
I seek enlightenment, with steady, measured pace.
In the realm of self-discovery, where emotions exhaust,
I confront hidden truths, no matter the cost.

In the recesses of my mind, where thoughts interlace,
I find self-awareness, in this enigmatic space.
In the realm of introspection, where insights embrace,
I confront my innermost demons, with courage and grace.

Chapter 64

Labyrinth of the Psyche: A Surreal Solitude

The narrator's feeling of being lost and alone

Within the Psychedelic Asylum's twisted corridors, I tread,
A surreal journey, psychiatric terms filling my head.
In my fractured psyche, confusion holds its sway,
Isolation and illness, in this realm, hold their play.

Amidst the shifting landscapes of my troubled mind,
Lost and alone, my thoughts intertwined.
"Solitude syndrome," and "existential estrangement" take their toll,
In this labyrinth of afflictions, I search for my soul.

"Why am I, the specter lost, in this desolate mental haze,
Adrift in my own afflictions, in this bewildering maze?"
My pondering echoes in a hallucinatory isolation,
Desolation profound, a haunting apparition's creation.

In this surreal dimension, my feelings become a fearful ride,
A nightmarish odyssey, in my own psyche, I'd confide.
Spectral apparitions dance through the corridors of my mind,
Echoes of emotional trauma, in this surreal world, I'd find.

Through this mental metaverse, thoughts take spectral form,
Phantasmagoric specters, in this surreal mental storm.
With isolation's weight, and the longing to be free,
I bridge the chasm within, between mind and reality.

Pressing onward, determined, in this psyche's desolate space,
To unearth solitude's essence, to confront the inner race.
In a realm of mental affliction, where terms held much power,
I face my own demons in this surreal, haunting hour.

In the labyrinth of the mind, I ventured without haste,
To fathom the solitude, in the depths of inner waste.
In the realm of introspection, where thoughts can devour,
I confronted my own shadows, in this psychological tower.

Through the maze of emotions, my quest was interlaced,
To grasp the solitude, in the mind's intricate embrace.
In the domain of self-reflection, where doubts often flower,
I faced my inner demons, in this psyche's darkest hour.

In the recesses of consciousness, where fears were interplaced,
I pursued solitude's secrets, in this enigmatic space.
In the realm of self-exploration, where thoughts could overpower,
I challenged my innermost shadows, in this psychological bower.

Within the corridors of the psyche, my journey was retraced,
To comprehend solitude's essence, in this internal chase.
In the world of introspection, where the mind can glower,
I wrestled with my own demons, in this mental tower.

Through the intricate passages of the mind, my path was traced,
Seeking solitude's meaning, in this internal landscape.
In the domain of self-discovery, where thoughts can devour,
I confronted my innermost shadows, in this psychological hour.

Chapter 65

Solitude's Labyrinth: A Surreal Odyssey Within

The narrator's fear of the unknown

In the twisting corridors of Psychedelic's eerie embrace,
A surreal journey unfolds, in the mind's mystic space.
Psychiatric terms weave a labyrinth, complex and obscure,
Within my fractured psyche, confusion's grip is sure.

Amid shifting landscapes of thoughts, a maelstrom of the mind,
I grapple with isolation, lost and confined.
"Solitude syndrome," and "existential estrangement" I hear,
Echoes in my thoughts, in this surreal atmosphere.

"Why am I the disoriented specter, lost in this desolation,
Adrift in my own afflictions, bound by isolation?"
I ponder, caught in a hallucinatory web's disarray,
Emotions reflect desolation, a haunting spectral display.

In this surreal dimension, I feel lost and alone,
A nightmarish odyssey, through mind's depths, I'm prone.
Spectral apparitions dance in corridors of trauma's brew,
Psychological complexity, in this realm, I construe.

Through this mental metaverse, my thoughts morph to specters grim,
Phantasmagoric echoes, in a surreal mental hymn.
Isolation's weight I bear, longing for connection's grace,
Bridging inner turmoil's chasm, yearning for a better place.

I press onward, determined, through this desolate abode,
To unearth solitude's essence, on a winding psyche road.
In this realm of affliction, where terms can hold much power,
I confront inner demons in this surreal, haunting hour.

In the depths of the subconscious, I ventured with resolve,
Seeking solitude's core, on a path my heart would absolve.
In the world of introspection, where fears can tower,
I faced my inner demons in this psychological bower.

Through the labyrinth of thoughts, my quest I'd often retrace,
To grasp solitude's essence, in the mind's intricate space.
In the realm of self-discovery, where doubts may flower,
I wrestled with my inner shadows in this psychological hour.

In the recesses of the psyche, where emotions interlace,
I pursued solitude's secrets, embracing its grace.
In the domain of self-exploration, where thoughts can glower,
I challenged my innermost demons in this mental tower.

Within the corridors of the mind, I'd find a hidden trace,
Hunting solitude's meaning, in this innermost place.
In the world of introspection, where fears tend to cower,
I confronted my inner demons during this psychological hour.

Through the intricate passages of the psyche, I'd embrace,
The essence of solitude, in this inner, sacred space.
In the realm of self-understanding, where thoughts can overpower,
I confronted my deepest shadows during this psychological hour.

Chapter 66

Labyrinth of the Mind: A Surreal Journey Within

The narrator's attempts to make sense of his surroundings

In the shadowed confines of the Psychedelic Asylum's night,
A surreal journey unfolds, bathed in eerie, dim light.
Psychiatric terms weave a cryptic, perplexing tapestry,
Within my fractured psyche, chaos and mystery.

Amidst shifting landscapes of thought, where uncertainty prevails,
I grapple relentlessly, as reality derails.
"Cognitive dissonance," "thought disorder," whispered in the air,
Entwined in my consciousness, a mental maze to bear.

"Why am I the fearless voyager in this cognitive labyrinth,
Seeking to decipher the enigma, a mind's intricate entrapment?"
I ponder, lost in a spectacle defying categorization,
My cognitive indices reflect turmoil, a maze of consternation.

Phantasmal apparitions of thoughts, in corridors, they dance,
In the cryptic language of psyche, they yearn to advance.
In this surreal dimension, comprehension remains untold,
Psychiatric terms eclipse clarity, in a world of stories untold.

Through this mental metaverse, my thoughts turn to riddles grand,
Elusive, ever-shifting, in this bewildering land.
A quest for understanding, in a language complex and obscure,
A profound need to decipher, my perception's inner allure.

I press onward with determination, through chaos I aspire,
To unveil the core of my turmoil, amidst thoughts that conspire.
In this realm of disarray, where words may wield much power,
I seek clarity in the shadows, in this surreal, enigmatic hour.

Through the labyrinthine corridors of my subconscious, I persist,
In the quest to fathom my inner turmoil, as shadows persist.
In the realm of mental tumult, where thoughts often tower,
I pursue lucidity within the shadows during this mysterious hour.

Amidst the intricate web of my psyche, I tread,
To fathom the heart of my unrest, where inner demons spread.
In this domain of cognitive disarray, where thoughts can overpower,
I strive for enlightenment in the shadows during this enigmatic hour.

In the recesses of my mind's abyss, I venture with care,
Exploring the depths of my turmoil, as inner voices declare.
In the world of psychological turbulence, where thoughts often glower,
I seek understanding within the shadows during this enigmatic hour.

Through the convoluted pathways of my subconscious, I roam,
Determined to decipher my inner chaos, as shadows loom.
In the realm of mental unrest, where thoughts have the power,
I search for clarity amidst the shadows during this mysterious hour.

Chapter 67

The Quest for the Enigmatic Woman in the Crimson Handbag

The narrator's reasons for following the woman

In a surreal dreamscape, where colors came alive,
I embarked on a quest, with a questor's drive.
I sought a woman, her allure hard to deny,
In the crimson handbag, beneath the dreamy sky.

She, the enigmatic siren, with cascading ebony strands,
In the monochrome world, like a rose, she stands.
Her grace, an elegant ballet, a dance so refined,
Her laughter, like crystalline notes, in my mind.

Reasons for pursuit, a kaleidoscope of shades,
Curiosity, fascination, desires in cascading cascades.
An inexplicable connection, reality it defied,
In my pursuit, in this dreamscape so wide.

The crimson handbag swung, a pendulum of fate,
As I ventured deeper, where reality and dreams equate.
Mysterious alleyways, kaleidoscopic scenes unfolded,
Adjectives painted my journey, tales yet untold.

In this hallucinatory realm, where illusions take flight,
The pursuit of the enigmatic, an odyssey so bright.
Surreal symphony of sights, sounds, and emotions untold,
Words danced like fireflies, in this dreamscape, bold.

Chasing adjectives that described her, I pressed on,
A journey of wonder, where reality was drawn.
Unlocking the essence of pursuit, in a surreal dance,
Where the enigmatic woman, in dreams, held a chance.

Chasing adjectives that painted her grace, I marched ahead,
In a wondrous odyssey, where reality's fabric seemed to spread.
Discovering the core of my quest, in a surreal trance,
Where the enigmatic woman's presence promised a chance.

Pursuing the words that defined her allure, I continued my quest,
In a wondrous voyage, where reality and dreams interwove their best.
Unveiling the heart of my pursuit, in an ethereal prance,
Where the enigmatic woman's enigma offered a mystical chance.

Hunting for adjectives that captured her mystique, I journeyed through,
In a wonder-filled adventure, where dreams and truth softly grew.
Revealing the soul of my chase, in a dreamlike circumstance,
Where the enigmatic woman beckoned with an alluring chance.

Chasing adjectives that embodied her mystery, I ventured far,
In a journey of wonder, where reality and dreams were ajar.
Unearthing the essence of my pursuit, in an entrancing advance,
Where the enigmatic woman's aura held a magical chance.

Pursuing the words that painted her intrigue, I persisted still,
In a wondrous expedition, where reality and dreams did distill.
Unlocking the heart of my quest, in a poetic romance,
Where the enigmatic woman's enigma offered a captivating chance.

Chapter 68

The Relentless Pursuit of the Crimson Handbag

The narrator's sense of urgency

In a surreal dreamscape, my odyssey took flight,
A pursuit of crimson enigma, urgency burning bright.
The world swirled in colors, otherworldly sounds abound,
A relentless, breathless chase, on surreal ground.

Urgency palpable, like a fevered, frantic drum,
Time itself capricious, moments rushing, some.
My heart pounded like thunderclaps, in my cavernous chest,
Pushing me forward, toward destiny's behest.

Seconds stretched to eternities, moments intense,
In this surreal realm, everything seemed immense.
The crimson handbag swung, marking each pace,
As I ventured forth, in this surreal chase.

Every footfall echoed, my breath drawn with anticipation,
A world of surrealism, each step a fascination.
Obstacles fantastical, in this dreamscape I faced,
Urgency my companion, in this surreal space.

In this labyrinth surreal, where reality's askew,
Urgency painted my journey, every hue anew.
A vivid, pulsating force, my senses did enhance,
Driven by urgency, in this surreal dance.

I pressed forward, determined and bold,
In this kaleidoscope of dreams, my story to unfold.
Unlocking the essence, of my pursuit's embrace,
Where adjectives danced, in this surreal chase.

With wonder in my eyes, I ventured forth,
Through the labyrinth of dreams, where surreal takes birth.
Embracing the enigma, my heart did race,
In this world of wonder, where dreams I'd chase.

Each adjective a stepping stone, to capture her essence,
In this wondrous pursuit, I felt no pretense.
Reality and illusion, a dance so intricate,
In my quest for wonder, I found the infinite.

A tapestry of adjectives, vivid and bright,
Woven in wonder, under starry night.
Each word a clue, in this enigmatic space,
Guiding me closer, in this captivating chase.

Through mazes of emotion, I'd bravely dive,
In the realm of wonder, where stories come alive.
With every twist and turn, I'd seek to embrace,
The essence of wonder, in this poetic race.

In the pursuit of wonder, I'd forge my own way,
In this kaleidoscope of dreams, I'd find my stay.
With wonder as my guide, I'd set the pace,
To unravel the mystery, in this wondrous chase.

Chapter 69

The Frustration of the Elusive Crimson

The narrator's frustration at not being able to find the woman

In a tapestry ever-shifting, my surreal quest unfurled,
Pursuing a phantom in crimson, in a perplexing world.
She remained elusive, a beguiling, wisp-like shade,
Each step a descent, where reality and illusion played.

Frustration surged like a tempest, an adjective-laden storm,
Emotions entwined, like a coiled spring taking form.
Exasperation and desperation, a turbulent sea,
In this surreal realm, where boundaries ceased to be.

Restless wanderer, ensnared in vexation's snare,
The labyrinth of my thoughts, a swirling, tangled affair.
In maddening mazes and fractal dreamscape's spree,
I sought to capture her essence, unravel the mystery.

In this hallucinatory domain, where emotions ran high,
Frustration was my companion, a relentless, vibrant cry.
A tempest of adjectives, swirling through the air,
In the labyrinth of my dreams, I continued to dare.

I pressed forward, relentless in my pursuit,
In this surreal symphony, where emotions took root.
Unlocking the essence, of vexation's embrace,
In a realm where adjectives danced, a surreal chase.

In this surreal odyssey, my spirits did swell,
Chasing elusive crimson in a vexing carousel.
Through frustration's tempest, I boldly strode,
In this world of wonder, where emotions flowed.

A symphony of adjectives, a maddening spree,
Entwined with exasperation, in a labyrinth so free.
Each step I took, in this twisting race,
Led deeper into vexation's maze, a perplexing place.

With relentless determination, I journeyed ahead,
Through the tempest of frustration, where confusion spread.
In the surreal realm of adjectives, I'd find my grace,
Unlocking the essence, in this enigmatic chase.

Chapter 70

The Enigma in Crimson's Dream

The narrator's thoughts and feelings about the woman

In the kaleidoscope, ever-shifting, she weaved her spell,
The woman in crimson, an enigma, who cast her mystic shell.
Her presence, a tantalizing contradiction, in this surreal space,
Mysterious yet alluring, a captivating, beguiling grace.

She danced as a mirage, her form a fluid, changing art,
A canvas of surreal beauty, an enigmatic work of heart.
My emotions swirled like a whirlpool, my thoughts a vivid stream,
In the labyrinth of my feelings, where adjectives formed a dream.

I, the enraptured dreamer, lost in her mesmerizing hold,
In a reverie where emotions and descriptions boldly unfold.
Fascination and frustration, desire and mystic perplexity,
A paradoxical enigma, defying surreal reality's decree.

Why was my connection with her a tapestry of vivid hues?
In this surreal realm, where every sentiment I'd choose.
Adjectives danced like apparitions, each a shade of our embrace,
In the ever-shifting landscape, I continued the dreamlike chase.

Forward I pressed, in this surreal pursuit, I strode,
Unlocking the essence of my connection with her down the vibrant,
adjective-laden road.
In a world where thoughts and feelings twirled in a trance,
I sought the enigma in crimson, my surreal, poetic romance.

I pressed forward, my spirit taking flight,
In this surreal journey, emotions burning bright.
Unlocking the essence of my connection with her, so grand,
Down the vibrant road of adjectives, hand in hand.

In a world of wonder, where feelings did dance,
I pursued the enigma of crimson, my chance.
With optimism as my guide, I embraced the trance,
Finding beauty and joy in this surreal romance.

Chapter 71

Whispers of the Temporal Rift

The narrator's surprise at finding the factory

Amidst the ethereal haze, I beheld a relic of time,
An old factory, timeworn, its presence quite sublime.
In a realm where illusions danced with the real,
This discovery, astonishing, a surreal narrative I'd feel.

It stood, ancient and grand, brick and rust entwined,
A portal to an era past, secrets waiting to be divined.
My astonishment, a symphony of awe and surprise,
Incredible wonder and disbelief mirrored in my eyes.

The factory, a silent behemoth, memories within its walls,
Of laborers long gone, echoing through its sepia halls.
"Why am I the humble wanderer," I mused in time's embrace,
Where past and present intertwined, in this enchanted place.

In this surreal realm, where time's sands rearranged,
Antiquity emerged, an unexpected, vivid change.
Every corner held secrets, astonishing discoveries to find,
As I pressed forward, with a curious mind.

My wonder, a guiding beacon, amidst this temporal rift,
Unveiling the essence of the factory, where history did uplift.
In a realm where workers' tales whispered in rhyme,
The surreal symphony of exploration continued through time.

My work, a timeless journey, in the factory's embrace,
Unveiling the essence of labor, where stories held their place.
In a realm where the clock's rhythm dictated the rhyme,
The surreal symphony of workers persisted through time.

Through shifts and tasks, in the factory's grand scheme,
I found meaning and purpose, like a recurring dream.
In the language of labor, where sweat and grit combined,
The essence of my efforts, a testament to humankind.

Chapter 72

Whispers of the Forgotten Factory

The narrator's sense of curiosity

In the midst of this surreal dream, where reality sways and twirls,
My curiosity, like a fire, unfurls.
An ancient factory, silent, stood as if in a trance,
Its aura whispered secrets, a timeless, enigmatic dance.

Curiosity, a blazing hearth, warming every thought's expanse,
"Why am I drawn," I pondered, as if in a rustic trance,
To this relic of the past, where time's whispers did declaim,
In the language of the workers, a forgotten history to reclaim.

In this surreal realm, where illusion intertwines with the real,
Curiosity was my torch, a guiding star to feel.
Deeper into the factory's heart, I ventured without fear,
Unraveling mysteries, as echoes of the past drew near.

Each step was a journey, through time's labyrinth I roamed,
A rusted cog, a faded signpost, hints of a past intoned.
Anticipation tingled, as I danced with history's ghost,
In this dreamscape where past and present coalesced the most.

I pressed onward, insatiable in my quest,
Curiosity my compass, guiding me through the rest.
Unlocking the factory's history, in a realm that defied the line,
English workers' tales whispered, transcending time's confine.

I pressed onward, fueled by work's grand lore,
Curiosity my compass, I explored the factory floor.
Unlocking the secrets of labor, in a realm where history shines,
English workers' stories whispered, transcending time's confines.

Amidst the clatter of machines and the rhythmic grind,
I unearthed the essence of work, in every story I'd find.
In the language of industry, where labor's sweat did intertwine,
The factory's legacy spoke, a testament to the human spine.

Chapter 73

Echoes of the Industrial Cathedral

The narrator's exploration of the factory

In dreams surreal and wide, I ventured forth,
On an exploration ride, to a forgotten north.
Into an ancient factory, where past and present meet,
In a surreal industry's dance, a symphony sweet.

Within its labyrinthine marvel, a cathedral made of steam,
Machines with names enchanting, like a distant, fading dream.
"Spindleweaver" and "Steamforged Behemoth" hold their sway,
In a realm where gears and pistons ruled, back in the bygone day.

On a pilgrimage of discovery, through annals long concealed,
Each step a chapter woven, by time's hand unsealed.
The symphony of machinery, the "Cogmaster's Choir" in the air,
A chorus of forgotten toil, echoing through the lair.

"Why am I the chronicler, in this grand industry's domain,
Where machines and workers' whispers craft a vivid, historic chain?"
My speech adorned with labor's lexicon, machines' arcane names,
As the factory itself bestows upon me, its storied claims.

In this surreal realm, where time's passage is askew,
My exploration, a captivating tale to pursue.
Deeper into the factory's heart, "Looming Serpents" at my side,
Carrying memories of ceaseless toil, on a conveyor belt ride.

Each discovery a revelation, machines stand as crafted sage,

A testament to craftsmanship from a bygone industrial age.

My senses enraptured, in this dreamscape's symphony I swirl,

An odyssey where past and present meet, and history unfurls.

I press forward, a tribute to workers old,

Their names and machines etched in a tale to be told.

Unlocking the essence of the factory's legacy,

In a realm where English workers whispered, in the echoing chambers of chance.

The Legacy Unveiled

I pressed forward, a tribute to workers old,

Their names and machines etched in a tale to be told.

Unlocking the essence of the factory's legacy, a surreal industry's dance,

In a realm where English workers whispered, in the echoing chambers of chance.

The Echoes of Labor

In this symphony of industry, I'd delve into the past,

As echoes of labor whispered, in memories vast.

Unearthing the stories, where dedication did enhance,

The essence of the factory, where workers took their stance.

The Machinery's Song

Amidst gears and cogs, I'd seek the heart's refrain,

Where machines once clattered, in the rhythm of gain.

Unlocking the secrets, in each mechanical advance,

The factory's history spoke, in a mechanical romance.

The Workers' Anthem

Through the dust and toil, I'd hear the workers' song,

In the language of labor, where dedication thronged.

Unveiling the legacy, where sweat and dreams did entrance,

The factory's tale unwound, in a workers' performance.

Chapter 74

Title: Echoes of the Industrial Reverie

The narrator's thoughts and feelings about the factory

In the embrace of a surreal reverie, my heart swelled
with admiration, nostalgia, and a connection that words could not
tell.
The factory, a testament to the ingenuity and grace of craftsmen,
stirred reverence in my soul as I explored its aged halls.

Its weathered walls and ancient machines, relics of days old,
whispered names of artisans, stories and history untold.
A symphony of emotions swirled within me, complex and deep: awe
and melancholy,
respect and longing woven into a tapestry.

"Why am I the reverent pilgrim in this grand industrial hall,
where spirits of workers and machines echo in history's thrall?"
I asked myself, my words adorned with labor's tongue and the
cherished names
of machines, as echoes of countless workers danced in spectral
frames.

In this surreal realm, where time flowed with an artist's brush,
the factory stood sentinel to days that did gently hush.
Thoughts and feelings painted scenes vivid and surreal,
a kinship with the machinery, a sense that time couldn't repeal.

Rusted cogs and faded signs sparked a nostalgia so clear,
a connection to the toilers who had labored year by year.
The factory, a symbol of resilience, craftsmanship, and art,
a monument to spirits strong, etched deep within the heart.

Amidst echoes of history, in a realm where time did sway,
I paid tribute to workers of another day.
Unlocking the essence of the factory's legacy in a dance so free,
where English workers whispered tales in the halls of industry's
spree.

The Crucible of Industry

Within the crucible of industry, where sweat and toil did thrive,
English workers forged a legacy, that still echoes alive.
With hearts of gold and hands of steel, they shaped the nation's
might,
In factories that hummed with life, both day and through the night.

Whispers of the Past

The walls of industry whisper tales, of workers brave and true,
Who toiled in mills and mines, their dreams forever new.
In accents rich and vibrant, their voices fill the air,
Echoing through the ages, with echoes of despair.

A Tapestry of Dreams

In the tapestry of industry, threads of workers' dreams entwine,
A symphony of voices, in a timeless refrain.
From the potter's wheel to the weaver's loom, their skills did shine,
A testament to human spirit, in the face of toil and time.

The Engine of Progress

The engine of progress roared ahead, on the wheels of workers' might,

As they fueled the furnace of industry, with sweat and all their might.

From cobblestone streets to towering mills, their hands built the nation's pride,

And in their hearts, a flame burned bright, a flame that couldn't hide.

A Legacy of Resilience

In the legacy of industry, English workers stand tall,

Their stories etched in history, their voices echoing through the hall.

Their spirit lives on in the factories they built,

A testament to their resilience, their strength, and their grit.

Chapter 75

The Odyssey of Self-Realization

The narrator's journey of self-discovery

In the ethereal labyrinth of dreams, where reality's grasp did slip,
I embarked on a quest, through thoughts and feelings, to equip
A journey of profound self-discovery, where revelations unfurled,
In the depths of my own psyche, where the secrets of the self were
twirled.

Epiphanies, like enigmatic blooms, within my mind did bloom,
From the inner sanctum of my soul, dispelling inner gloom.
Each realization, a puzzle piece, a mosaic of my essence,
A voyage steeped in introspection, a journey of significance.

"Cur ego sum qui quaero semet ipsum in hoc mirabili somnio?"
I contemplated, my Latin words bathed in ancient wisdom's bestow.
In this surreal realm, self-realizations gleamed like torchlight's
glow,
A dance of inner dialogue, where the subconscious seeds did sow.

Within the kaleidoscope of thought, the threads of self I'd weave,
Unraveling facets hidden deep, in shadows I'd retrieve.
Latin phrases etched in mind, as wisdom from the ages soared,
Ancient whispers in my ear, profound truths to be explored.

Desires and fears, complexities unveiled, conscious and unconscious lay bare,
A journey into my very core, where self-knowledge was my fare.
In this hallucinatory realm, where reality and introspection intertwined,
Self-realizations painted a portrait, the depths of self I'd find.

I pressed onward, guided by the star of self-awareness,
In the surreal symphony of introspection, I'd seek the truth's fairness.
Unlocking the essence of identity, in corridors of psyche's grandeur,
In a realm where meaning's hidden, in self-realization's splendor.

The Quest for Clarity

I pressed onward, guided by the star of self-awareness,
In the surreal symphony of introspection, I'd seek the truth's fairness.
Unlocking the essence of my identity, in corridors of my psyche's grandeur,
In a realm where meaning's hidden, in self-realization's splendor.

Shadows of Self

In the labyrinth of my thoughts, I'd confront shadows that loom,
In the quest for self-awareness, where darkness met the room.
Unveiling the layers, where my identity's nuances did entrance,
In a battle against burnout, I'd seek my self's resilience.

Embracing the Inner Chaos

Amidst the chaos within, I'd find my heart's refrain,

In the language of emotions, where empathy did gain.

Unlocking the turmoil, where authenticity took its stance,

In a realm of introspection, I'd confront the inner dance.

The Symphony of Self-Discovery

Through the cacophony of doubts, I'd hear my inner song,

In the rhythm of self-discovery, where authenticity belonged.

Unearthing my essence, in moments of introspective trance,

In the symphony of identity, I'd find a second chance.

The Rebirth of Self

In the crucible of reflection, I'd emerge anew,

In the fires of self-awareness, where insights grew.

Rekindling my essence, where resilience did enhance,

In the rebirth of self, I'd find my balanced stance.

Chapter 76

The Metamorphosis of Self-Discovery

The narrator's realizations about himself

In the fantastical realm where dreams did sway,
I embarked on a journey, night and day.
A profound process of growth and change, in a tapestry unfurled,
My evolution of self, in a surreal, conscious world.

Metamorphosis, like a butterfly in flight,
Transcended boundaries, took me to great height.
Through the surreal landscape, my psyche I'd unfurl,
In the labyrinth of self, a transformation did swirl.

"Cresco et evolvo, sicut pupa que in papilionem mutatur,"
Latin phrases whispered wisdom, ancient and pure.
In this realm, my growth illuminated, self-awareness shone,
A journey into depths of soul, a self-discovery of my own.

Beliefs, desires, fears, all laid bare with clarity's grace,
Layers of the subconscious, like an ancient manuscript's embrace.
Each revelation, a Latin axiom etched with profound insight,
The essence of my growth, a language of wisdom, bright.

In this hallucinatory domain, where reality and introspection wed,
My evolution, through psychology's lens, I'd tread.
A dreamscape where expressions of self, timeless and grand,
Merged in surreal symphony, personal growth's vibrant band.

I pressed onward, my growth a guiding star,

In this surreal narrative, I journeyed near and far.

Unlocking the essence of development, where meanings softly sighed,

In enigmatic corridors of psyche's depths, my self did bide.

Navigating the Skillset Spectrum

I pressed onward, my growth a guiding star,

In this surreal narrative, I journeyed near and far.

Unlocking the essence of development, where skills intertwined,

In enigmatic corridors of learning, expertise I'd find.

The Labyrinth of Competence

Through mazes of knowledge, I'd navigate the way,

In this world of competencies, where experts held sway.

Unveiling the layers, where proficiency did dance,

In the quest for mastery, I'd take every chance.

Elevation in the Skill Matrix

Amidst the ranks of aptitude, I'd rise and shine,

In the matrix of skills, where expertise did align.

Unlocking the potential, where excellence had a stance,

In a realm of development, I'd seize every circumstance.

The Symphony of Proficiency

Through the notes of competence, I'd hear my own song,

In the rhythm of expertise, where abilities belong.

Unearthing the essence, in moments of insightful glance,

In the symphony of skills, I'd continue to advance.

The Renaissance of Capability

In the crucible of growth, I'd emerge full-grown,

In the fires of development, where wisdom's seeds were sown.

Rekindling my potential, where aptitude would enhance,

In the renaissance of abilities, I'd continue to dance.

Chapter 77

The Illumination of Self-Acceptance

The narrator's growth and development

Amidst surreal reverie, I reached a vital shore,
A moment of self-acceptance, enlightenment's core.
In this realm of self-discovery, a dance did ensue,
Adorned with Latin phrases, wisdom old and true.

My self-acceptance, a revelation, a radiant light,
Recognizing my worth and identity, shining so bright.
Through surreal corridors of self, I did roam,
Embracing every aspect, finding a sacred home.

"Cognosco et amo me ipsum," I whispered with grace,
Latin phrases carried wisdom from an ancient place.
In this ethereal domain, self-acceptance did gleam,
With the radiant light of understanding, like a dream.

Flaws and imperfections, I came to adore,
Integral parts of my being, I did explore.
Each realization, a Latin aphorism, a profound view,
Etched upon the tapestry, wisdom old and true.

In this hallucinatory realm, where introspection did blend,
My self-acceptance, a journey without end.
Through a dreamscape where psychology and expressions collide,
A surreal symphony of growth, self-love as my guide.

I pressed forward, self-acceptance in tow,

In the surreal narrative of self, I'd continue to grow.

Unlocking newfound understanding in corridors of the mind,

In this enigmatic realm, a story of acceptance intertwined.

Embracing the Self-Discovery Quest

I pressed forward, self-acceptance in tow,

In the surreal narrative of self, I'd continue to grow.

Unlocking newfound understanding in corridors of the mind,

In this enigmatic realm, a story of acceptance intertwined.

The Self-Reflection Chronicles

Through mirrors of introspection, I'd gaze without fear,

In the reflections of self, both far and near.

Unveiling the layers of identity, where emotions intertwined,

In the quest for authenticity, I'd explore my mind.

The Identity Integration Symphony

Amidst the orchestration of self, I'd harmonize and play,

In the symphony of identity, where emotions had their say.

Unlocking the potential for wholeness, where soul and self combined,

In a realm of self-acceptance, I'd align.

The Dance of Personal Growth

Through the steps of transformation, I'd waltz and sway,

In the dance of self-discovery, where truths held sway.

Unearthing the essence of authenticity, with every step I'd bind,

In the ballet of acceptance, I'd continue to find.

The Artistry of Inner Peace

In the canvas of inner landscapes, I'd paint my own scene,

In the masterpiece of self, where tranquility gleamed.

Reveling in the brushstrokes of self-compassion, love defined,

In the gallery of acceptance, I'd peacefully recline.

Chapter 78

The Shifting Badge of Identity

The narrator's search for a sense of identity

In the cosmic realm of corporate prose,

Where buzzwords bloomed and jargon flows,

I drifted, my identity askew,

A holographic badge, an ever-changing hue.

Through endless meetings, data's siren song,

I pondered where I truly did belong.

A data point on scatterplots confined,

Or something more, a unique corporate mind?

Then came a day, a presentation's twist,

Where bar graphs danced and buzzwords kissed.

The world transformed, a river shimmered bright,

And cryptic riddles replaced the boardroom's light.

I saw myself as quite unique,

An outlier bold, no longer meek.

A disruptor's role, I yearned to claim,

In this surreal wonderland, I'd stake my name.

To pivot from conformity's embrace,

To navigate this strange and shifting space,

I embarked on a quest, a corporate odyssey,

Seeking my true self in algorithms' symphony.

Through corridors of innovation, I'd explore,

In search of something worth striving for.

A journey surreal, in dreams and data's grasp,

To find my identity, an elusive, shifting clasp.

In this realm of business dreams untold,

Where buzzwords and jargon took their hold,

My quest, a mesmerizing dance,

Challenged the norms of corporate circumstance.

So, let us delve into this tale profound,

In the corporate cosmos, where truths are found.

A journey of identity, both strange and grand,

In the Halls of Buzzwords, where surreal dreams expand.

The Spreadsheet Symphony

In the columns and rows of data's embrace,

I toiled and typed, in this corporate space.

Unlocking the essence of productivity's demand,

In the Spreadsheet Symphony, where numbers command.

The Meeting Room Mirage

Amidst conference calls and meetings galore,

I sought recognition, my voice to restore.

Unveiling the essence of work's endless hand,

In the Meeting Room Mirage, where decisions withstand.

The Deadline Dilemma

Through the pressure and stress of looming tasks,

I navigated deadlines, with courage unmasked.

Unearthing the essence of burnout's cruel brand,

In the Deadline Dilemma, where time slips through sand.

The Office Oasis

In the midst of it all, I'd find a retreat,

An Office Oasis, where exhaustion I'd beat.

Reveling in moments of relief, as the clock's hands expand,

In the pursuit of balance, where dreams withstand.

Chapter 79

Chapter of Virtual Dreams

The narrator's desire to find a place where he belongs

In this chapter of virtual dreams, I tread,
Through bytes and bits, where purpose lies,
In meetings endless, corporate jargon spread,
A lost algorithm, I yearn to rise.

One day, a vision strange did me befall,
The office walls to buzzword forests turned,
A portal in the room, a beckoning call,
To realms surreal, where knowledge churned.

I ventured forth, in data's wild domain,
Chatbots in riddles spoke, a cryptic tongue,
Cyborg colleagues measured praise and gain,
 In likes and shares, their digital song sung.

My quest took flight, to pixelated lands,
Where code and graphics danced in unity,
A virtual oasis, where AI stands,
For belonging found in digital community.

In this surreal landscape, dreams took flight,
Identity and purpose, I did explore,
A whimsical journey, surreal and bright,
In the ever-evolving world of business, I sought more.

The Career Canvas

In this surreal landscape, dreams took flight,

As I painted my career, both day and night.

Navigating the canvas of ambition's grand lore,

In the Career Canvas, where aspirations soar.

With every brushstroke, my vision grew clear,

A roadmap to success, a path to hold dear.

I blended my skills and passions with care,

Crafting a masterpiece, beyond compare.

The Success Symposium

Identity and purpose, I did explore,

In a Success Symposium, I'd learn and implore.

Networking and mentoring, knowledge I'd pour,

In this world of strategy, where careers galore.

I listened to the stories of those who had paved the way,

And learned from their wisdom, day by day.

I forged connections, built relationships deep,

In this supportive space, where dreams did leap.

The Performance Paradox

A whimsical journey, surreal and bright,

Yet I faced a paradox, a challenging fight.

Performance metrics and goals to restore,

In the Performance Paradox, I'd strive for more.

I learned to balance the demands of my role,
While staying true to my authentic soul.
I embraced the challenges, and grew from each test,
In the Performance Paradox, I gave my best.

The Feedback Fandango

In the ever-evolving world of business, I sought more,
Feedback and growth, my spirits would soar.
Constructive criticism and praise to explore,
In the Feedback Fandango, I'd embrace the score.

I welcomed feedback with an open heart,
Knowing it was the key to setting me apart.
I learned from my mistakes, and celebrated my wins,
In the Feedback Fandango, my progress did spin.

The Leadership Labyrinth

Through leadership roles, I'd chart my course,
In the corporate labyrinth, a formidable force.
Influence and vision, my skills to the fore,
In the Leadership Labyrinth, I'd rise and explore.

I empowered others, and inspired teamwork,
Navigating the labyrinth, with a strategic gleam.
I embraced the challenges, and thrived in the maze,
In the Leadership Labyrinth, my legacy I'd blaze.

Chapter 80

Outsider's Odyssey: Navigating Corporate Wonderland

The challenges of feeling like an outsider

In the midst of virtual meetings, algorithms, and screens,
I wandered through surreal corporate dreams.
A digital maze of buzzwords and code I'd explore,
Seeking belonging, a place to fit in, and more.

Each day, the boardroom, a holographic domain,
Where charts pirouetted, in a dance far from plain.
Colleagues became avatars, faces unknown,
In a landscape where data and jargon were thrown.

But I felt different, like an outsider lost,
A glitch in the system, at a great digital cost.
Emails vanished in bytes, a startup so small,
In a world of tech giants, I couldn't stand tall.

Then, one day, a twist, in a virtual embrace,
I entered a realm where words took on grace.
Sentient spreadsheets debated, chatbots found their voice,
In a surreal terrain where corporate jargon was choice.

As I ventured through this fantastical land,
I realized my difference was a strength, understand.
Unique perspectives, ideas that would soar,
In the chaos, I found what I'd been searching for.

In this surreal domain where language took flight,
My challenge transformed to a light.
A beacon of innovation, a creative finesse,
In Corporate Wonderland, I found my true address.

The Lexicon Odyssey
In this surreal domain where language took flight,
I embarked on a Lexicon Odyssey, both day and night.
Mastering buzzwords and phrases, a linguistic prowess,
In Corporate Wonderland, I'd navigate this linguistic excess.

From "actionable insights" to "synergistic solutions,"
I learned to speak the corporate tongue, with all its confusions.
I decoded cryptic emails and jargon-filled reports,
Unraveling the mysteries of this lexical labyrinth's courts.

The Paradigm Puzzle
The outsider's challenge transformed to a light,
Solving the Paradigm Puzzle, I'd reach new heights.
Restructuring and shifting, with strategy to impress,
In Corporate Wonderland, I'd decode this enigmatic mess.

I embraced the ever-changing landscape,
its paradigms so vast, Adapting to new realities, my mind surpassed.
I crafted innovative solutions, with insights profound,
In the Paradigm Puzzle, my brilliance would be resound.

The Synergy Symphony
A beacon of innovation, a creative finesse,
I composed a Synergy Symphony, to impress.

Harmonizing ideas, merging concepts no less,

In Corporate Wonderland, I'd create a potent synthesis.

I collaborated with diverse minds, our talents entwined,

Weaving a tapestry of brilliance, one of a kind.

We forged new paths, transcending boundaries untold,

In the Synergy Symphony, our magic did unfold.

The Networking Nexus

In this surreal landscape of career finesse,

I explored the Networking Nexus, a realm to address.

Connections and contacts, my influence would progress,

In Corporate Wonderland, I'd build a robust fortress.

I nurtured relationships, with genuine intent,

Building a network of allies, on which to cement.

My authenticity shone, in this digital domain,

In the Networking Nexus, my impact I'd sustain.

The Performance Paradiso

Amidst challenges and buzzwords, I'd remain upright,

Conquering the Performance Paradiso, shining so bright.

Metrics and targets, my efforts to express,

In Corporate Wonderland, I'd achieve success.

I set ambitious goals, and soared with determination,

Embracing the journey, with passion and elation.

I celebrated my wins, and learned from my mistakes,

In the Performance Paradiso, my legacy I'd make.

Chapter 81

The Odyssey of Meaning Amidst Pixels

The narrator's search for meaning in life

Amid the digital chaos, I set forth on a quest,
To find meaning in bytes, to be my very best.
In the corporate maelstrom, I felt quite bereft,
Seeking purpose profound, where meaning was left.

Through mazes of jargon, I forged my own way,
In a world full of buzzwords, I'd find brighter day.
KPIs and metrics, like a dense forest they grew,
Yet deep down inside, there was something I knew.

One day, a screensaver, a vision so grand,
An iceberg emerged, like a dream from the sand.
A mountain it turned, reaching high to the sky,
I knew I must climb, with purpose awry.

Each step was a metaphor, a lesson, a clue,
In the fog of illusions, my purpose I'd pursue.
Quarterly reports, a mere fragment of whole,
Life's meaning was found in a much deeper goal.

Connections with others, the impact I'd make,
In the digital realm, these were real, not fake.
Collaboration's sweet moments, amidst the noise's descent,
Were the gems of my journey, the moments well-spent.

In surreal illusions, where metaphors took flight,

My quest for true meaning, a beacon of light.

Life's purpose was complex, like a multifaceted gem,

In the midst of the chaos, I'd find it in them.

In this digital domain, where illusions would twirl,

I pursued my true purpose, a transformative whirl.

For amidst all the pixels and jargon's refrain,

I'd find meaning and purpose, in a world so surreal and plain.

The Quest for Purposeful Pixels

In this digital domain, where illusions would twirl,

I embarked on a quest for Purposeful Pixels, a purposeful swirl.

Seeking depth amidst shallow data's endless drain,

In Corporate Wonderland, I'd find meaning for which I'd strain.

The Enigma of Work's Purpose

For amidst all the pixels and jargon's refrain,

I delved into the Enigma of Work's Purpose, undeterred by the strain.

Unraveling the mysteries, in this corporate terrain,

In Corporate Wonderland, I'd decode what seemed arcane.

The Symposium of Significance

I continued the journey, the pursuit remained,

In the Symposium of Significance, where I gained.

Insights and wisdom, my efforts not in vain,

In Corporate Wonderland, meaning would no longer wane.

The Purpose-Driven Perspective

Seeking depth and purpose, I'd forge a meaningful chain,

Adopting a Purpose-Driven Perspective, my course to sustain.

Aligning values and goals, like a poetic refrain,

In Corporate Wonderland, my mission I'd ascertain.

The Fulfillment Finale

In this surreal world, I'd grow and train,

Towards the Fulfillment Finale, I'd break the chain.

No more pixelated pursuits, no more mundane,

In Corporate Wonderland, meaning and purpose would reign.

Chapter 82

The Odyssey of Purpose Amidst Jargon

The importance of finding purpose in life

In the corporate whirlwind, I set sail,
Seeking purpose profound, through jargon's thick veil.
A virtual boardroom, spreadsheets in flight,
Data danced in the air, like a spectral light.

"Amidst ROI, KPIs, what's my true quest?"
My voice merged with jargon, a surreal bequest.
Phantom colleagues replied, but answers did blur,
In the midst of the buzzwords, I'd seek to confer.

Deeper I ventured, a hidden door found,
A room bathed in light, where purpose was crowned.
"Make a Difference," the walls seemed to say,
"Leave a Legacy," in the lexicon's sway.

In the corporate whirlwind, where meetings took flight,
Purpose was the beacon, a guiding star's light.
Amidst buzzwords and jargon, a diamond would gleam,
In the heart of my quest, it fulfilled my grand dream.

In this surreal realm, where illusions took hold,
Purpose was my treasure, more precious than gold.
A narrative meaningful, amidst jargon's grand scope,
I'd find it within, and fill life's bright envelope.

In pursuit of my purpose, I forged my own way,

Through the buzzwords and meetings, I'd seize the day. I

n the surreal corporate landscape, my journey took flight,

To find my own meaning, a beacon of light.

Navigating the Labyrinth of Meaning

I forged my own way,

navigating the Labyrinth of Meaning, where clarity did sway.

Through the buzzwords and meetings, I'd seize the day's delight,

In Corporate Wonderland's puzzle, I'd seek what's right.

The Quest for Significance

In the surreal corporate landscape, my journey took flight,

The Quest for Significance, my guiding light.

Among data streams and meetings, I'd find my might,

In Corporate Wonderland's paradox, I'd redefine the night.

The Harmonious Workplace Symphony

Through the symphony of jargon, I'd engage in the fight,

To create a Harmonious Workplace Symphony, an inspiring sight.

Balancing metrics and teamwork, day and night,

In Corporate Wonderland's rhythm, I'd find my insight.

The Path to Purposeful Productivity

Amidst deadlines and pressure, I'd shine so bright,

On the Path to Purposeful Productivity, I'd take flight.

Unlocking my potential, like stars in the corporate height,

In Corporate Wonderland's journey, I'd discover my might.

Chapter 83

The Enigma of Meaning Amidst Jargon

The difficulty of finding meaning in a world that often seems meaningless

I navigated the corporate realm, where corridors entwine,
With jargon's cryptic language, a riddle divine.
Endless reports, charts that seemed to transcend,
In the surreal data, where meanings suspend.

Pie charts, bar graphs, like phantoms they soared,
Whispering data, a mystic rapport.
In the maze of buzzwords, a language so dense,
I pondered, my voice intense.

"Why chase these metrics, these bottom-line themes,
Lost in the jargon of profit and dreams?"
My words echoed through data, as colleagues opine,
In surreal mantras, of markets they dine.

Navigating this landscape, bewildering and strange,
I stumbled upon a door, a doorway to change.
In a room bathed in light, iridescent and bright,
Phrases adorned walls, like stars in the night.

"Seek Fulfillment," and "Unlock the Meaning" in flight,
Cryptic script of purpose, in the room's gentle light.
The challenge was clear, in a world so absurd,
Finding meaning 'midst jargon, like seeking a word.

In this surreal realm, where illusions do play,

My quest for true purpose, a path to convey.

Amidst corporate cacophony, like a cosmic riddle's gleam,

The meaning I sought, like a surreal dream.

I pressed ever forward, the quest to unfold,

In a world often vacant of meaning, so cold.

Through the buzzwords and data, my journey took flight,

To find my own purpose, like a beacon of light.

The Quest for Purpose

I pressed ever forward, the Quest for Purpose in sight,

In the corporate landscape's labyrinth, where goals took flight.

Through KPIs and metrics, my journey felt right,

To find my unique purpose, a guiding star so bright.

Unveiling the Purpose Paradox

Amidst the paradox of meaning and corporate might,

Unveiling the Purpose Paradox, my heart alight.

Balancing work and passion, with all of my might,

In the surreal corporate dance, I'd search for insight.

The Symphony of Work and Passion

Through the symphony of work and passion, I'd unite,

Harmonizing productivity with purpose, what a sight!

In the realm of business, where days turned into night,

I'd discover my calling, in the Purpose's golden light.

Chapter 84

Hope's Illumination in the Corporate Mirage

The narrator's hope for a better future

I navigated the corporate dreamscape, surreal and wide,
Hope shone through jargon's relentless tide.
Meetings and memos, a maze to explore,
In the hallucination of work, I yearned for more.

Hope, like a beacon, in a haze did gleam,
A KPI of sanity in this abstract dream.
"Why persist in this dance, this jargon ballet,
If not to create a brighter, meaningful day?"

My words echoed through slides, a surreal array,
In the landscape of visions, I found my own way.
Through metaphors and budgets, conflicting and wild,
Hope was my anchor, my reason, my guide.

In this bewildering realm where illusions did spin,
I found a surreal portal, a gateway within.
To a room bathed in light, serene and profound,
Phrases on walls, with hope's wisdom they're crowned.

"Resilience Breeds Progress," and "The Future Awaits,"
In the lexicon of hope, where no challenge abates.
I realized in jargon's midst, where confusion unfurled,
Hope was the compass, the map to my world.

In the dance of hallucination, hope led the way,
A testament to my spirit, come what may.
Amidst business's maze, with dreams surreal,
Hope and determination forged a narrative, real.

I pressed ever forward, on hope's gentle stream,
Shaping a future that's more than it seemed.
In the corporate labyrinth, where surreal meets the real,
Hope and resilience unlocked my surreal ideal.

Navigating the Streams of Purpose

I pressed ever forward, on life's grand scheme,
Navigating the Streams of Purpose, like a dream.
In the corporate labyrinth, where data's the keel,
Purposeful ambitions revealed what was concealed.

Finding Purpose Amidst Chaos

Amidst the chaos of the corporate regime,
Finding Purpose Amidst Chaos, my new regime.
Balancing ambitions and daily corporate ordeal,
I sought clarity in the Purpose's ideal.

The Symphony of Life's Purpose

Through the Symphony of Life's Purpose, I'd gleam,
Creating a life that's more than just a scheme.
In the world of business, where decisions did seal,
I discovered the symphony, my own surreal.

Chapter 85

Resilience's Triumph in the Corporate Mirage

The narrator's ability to overcome challenges

In the realm of illusions, where corporate dreams sway,
I faced challenges surreal, each passing day.
A maze of buzzwords, a cryptic terrain,
I pondered my purpose in this jargon's domain.

"Am I the trailblazer?" I questioned the scheme,
 In the labyrinth of KPIs, an abstract dream.
Through paradigms that shifted, reality askew,
I sought innovation amidst visions anew.

"Synergistic endeavors" in ethereal dance,
A surreal odyssey, a complex trance.
Disruptive technologies, altering sight,
In the language of business, I fought through the night.

Resilience, my armor, in the jargon's embrace,
With "agile thinking," I quickened my pace.
"Strategic planning," my sword in the fight,
I harnessed expertise to bring clarity to light.

Cross-functional prowess, a compass so true,
In "change management" waves, I skillfully grew.
With each surreal challenge, I rose to the task,
Unraveling puzzles behind a business-like mask.

In this metaverse surreal, where trials did unfurl,

My resilience, a transformative whirl.

Amidst jargon's complex and bewildering scene,

I found the key to deciphering what life could mean.

With unwavering determination, I ventured each mile,

Ready for challenges in the corporate dreamscape's style.

Armed with language and resilience to confront the unknown,

I pressed ever forward, my strength brightly shown.

The Quest for Purposeful Clarity

With unwavering determination, I embarked on this trial,

In The Quest for Purposeful Clarity, I'd compile.

Through the corporate maze, where aspirations are sown,

I sought clear life purpose, seeds of purpose freshly grown.

Purposeful Strategies in the Corporate Domain

Navigating the corporate domain, mile by mile,

Crafting Purposeful Strategies with an innovative smile.

In this landscape of strategy, where visions were honed,

I forged a path to purpose, my aspirations finely honed.

Purpose-Driven Decisions in the Boardroom

In the boardroom's power, I'd take every file,

Making Purpose-Driven Decisions with a determined guile.

Among executives' debates, where influence was overblown,

I carved a purposeful path, in the corporate world's zone.

Chapter 86

Hope's Resilience in the Corporate Mirage

The importance of hope in the face of adversity

In the corridors surreal, where illusions held sway,
I found hope in a jargon-filled day.
A kaleidoscope dream, with buzzwords so grand,
In this cosmic dance, hope was my guiding hand.

"Why am I the optimist?" I pondered the scene,
In this labyrinth of jargon, where words intervened.
Market volatility, like storms in the night,
Strategic alignment, celestial bodies in flight.

With each surreal challenge, a puzzle, a quest,
I clung to my hope, found it to be best.
A hostile takeover by towering chess piece,
Hope kept me steadfast, my worries did cease.

ROI optimization, a shifting chart's plan,
Through the desert of data, hope was my fan.
An ember, a spark, in the surreal abyss,
It fueled my resilience in a world so remiss.

In this metaverse strange, where adversity played,
Hope's importance was clear, like the sun's golden braid.
A driving force, a light in the dark,
Through business's maze, it left its bright mark.

I pressed on undeterred, in this mirage's ballet,

Hope by my side in the corporate melee.

Armed with business jargon, with hope as my guide,

I ventured ahead, with nothing to hide.

Navigating Purpose Amid Corporate Waves

I ventured ahead in this corporate ballet,

Navigating Purpose Amid Corporate Waves, come what may.

With resilience as my compass, and values to confide,

I embarked on this journey, my purpose as my guide.

Purposeful Strategies in the Business Arena

In the business arena, I'd brightly convey,

Purposeful Strategies, leading the way.

With mission statements clear, in the corporate tide,

I shaped my destiny, with purpose as my guide.

The Symphony of Purposeful Leadership

In leadership's realm, where I'd often sway,

The Symphony of Purposeful Leadership would hold sway.

With vision and ethics, through the corporate divide,

I inspired my team, with purpose as my guide.

Purpose-Fueled Innovation in a Changing World

In a changing world, where conditions could betray,

Purpose-Fueled Innovation, a guiding ray.

With creativity and ethics, in the corporate ride,

I forged new pathways, with purpose as my guide.

Chapter 87

Embracing the Mirage: A Journey of Self-Acceptance

The narrator's journey of self-acceptance

In the surreal realm where corporate dreams reside,
I embarked on a quest, my heart as my guide.
A journey profound, through buzzwords and more,
In this labyrinthine world, acceptance I'd explore.

"Why am I the outlier?" I questioned the scene,
In this corporate dreamscape, where facades intervene.
Strategic pivots and metrics, a chaotic terrain,
Amongst fluctuating values, my self I'd regain.

In a world where transparency was a phantom so fleet,
And accountability seemed like a distant heartbeat,
Self-acceptance became a journey of grace,
Amidst surreal jargon, I'd find my own place.

With each step I took, self-discovery unfurled,
A dance with my values in this surreal world.
To align aspirations with the corporate dream's seam,
Self-acceptance was vital, my guiding moonbeam.

In this metaverse strange, where doubts took their flight,
Self-doubt's surreal challenges, I'd conquer the night.
Forgiveness, I'd learn, starts within one's own heart,
Embracing my quirks was the place to restart.

I pressed on undaunted, authenticity my creed,

In the corporate dreamscape, where illusions did breed.

Unlocking forgiveness, compassion's true art,

Amidst buzzwords and balance sheets, I'd find my own part.

In this narrative surreal, my journey's embrace,

Of self-acceptance's essence, in this corporate dreamscape.

A beacon of authenticity in the surreal corporate scheme,

A testament to resilience, my journey's grand theme.

Self-Discovery Amid Corporate Mirage

Amid the corporate mirage, where facades interlace,

I embarked on a quest for Self-Discovery Amid Corporate Mirage.

With self-awareness as my compass, I'd boldly scheme,

To uncover my true self, in this surreal corporate dream.

Authentic Leadership in the Business Odyssey

In the business odyssey, where roles interlace,

Authentic Leadership became my guiding star in this space.

With vulnerability as my power, I'd strive to redeem,

The true essence of leadership, in this surreal corporate dream.

The Symphony of Self-Acceptance

In the symphony of life, where notes do interlace,

The Symphony of Self-Acceptance became my defining grace.

With authenticity as my anthem, I'd boldly deem,

That embracing my uniqueness was the essence of the dream.

Chapter 88

Forging Unity: The Power of Forgiveness in the Corporate Odyssey

The narrator's ability to forgive others

In the surreal realm where meetings took flight,
I embarked on a journey, a quest for true sight.
Forgiveness, I found, was a key to success,
In this corporate landscape, it set my soul at rest.

Amidst "synergy" and alliances, I pondered and saw,
In a world of ambition, where competition was raw,
"Why am I the enlightened one?" I would say,
Where forgiveness was vital, to light up the way.

My path was adorned with surreal encounters untold,
Colleagues turned concepts, where mysteries unfold.
Office politics danced, enigmatic and grand,
In these moments surreal, forgiveness took a stand.

In this world where the ladder seemed endless and wide,
"Win-win scenarios" were dreams on the tide,
Forgiveness emerged as a tool of great might,
Bridging gaps, dissolving conflicts, shining bright.

Through the maze of "stakeholder engagement" I'd roam,
In "strategic vision" I'd find my true home.
Forgiving, I'd rise above corporate's grim theme,
In this surreal narrative, unity my grand scheme.

My ability to forgive, a strategic embrace,

In the corporate odyssey's surreal, tangled space.

Unlocking compassion, where buzzwords would wane,

In this corporate cosmos, forgiveness would reign.

Forgiveness in the Heart of Corporate Complexity

Amidst corporate complexity, where masks I'd efface,

Forgiveness in the Heart of Corporate Complexity, my chosen grace.

Unlocking compassion's power, where conflicts may stain,

In this corporate cosmos, forgiveness begins its reign.

The Art of Reconciliation in the Business Ballet

In the business ballet, where conflicts oft interlace,

The Art of Reconciliation, my harmonious embrace.

Unlocking understanding's door, where disputes leave a chain,

In this corporate cosmos, forgiveness's healing shall sustain.

Forgiveness: The Cornerstone of Ethical Leadership

On the path of leadership, where moral choices interlace,

Forgiveness: The Cornerstone of Ethical Leadership, my moral base.

Unlocking ethical principles, where integrity I retain,

In this corporate cosmos, forgiveness's ethics remain.

Forgiveness: The Currency of Trust in Corporate Realms

In corporate realms, where trust I'd embrace,

Forgiveness: The Currency of Trust in Corporate Realms, my
chosen grace.

Unlocking trust's foundation, where trustworthiness I maintain,

In this corporate cosmos, forgiveness builds trust's domain.

Chapter 89

Embracing Grace: The Surreal Symphony of Acceptance and Forgiveness

The importance of acceptance and forgiveness in life

In the corporate dreamscape, my journey took flight,
Revealing a truth, shining clear and bright.
Acceptance and forgiveness, their essence so grand,
In the theater of life, where connections are planned.

Through "strategic planning" and objectives I'd delve,
"Why am I awakened?" I thought to myself.
In this intricate dance of human connection's embrace,
Acceptance and forgiveness, the keys to the chase.

My path wound through corridors surreal and obscure,
Colleagues became concepts, dramas obscure.
Office politics played, like Shakespeare's grand theme,
Acceptance and forgiveness, in life's complex scheme.

In a world where success often shrouded the true,
Existence's essence, a surreal avenue.
Acceptance, I found, was the bond that we share,
Imperfections acknowledged, connections laid bare.

Deeper I ventured, through growth's twisting vine,
"Emotional intelligence," a concept divine.
Forgiveness, I learned, was the balm that we need,
A bridge between souls, in humanity's creed.

I pressed forward, unwavering, my mission so bright,

In life's surreal narrative, a beacon of light.

Unlocking compassion, understanding's embrace,

In a world full of buzzwords, I found my own grace.

Compassion's Role in the Corporate Orchestra

In the corporate orchestra, where ambitions take flight,

I embarked on a journey, to shed some light.

Compassion's role, I sought to explore,

In this corporate symphony, where it played a key role.

Compassion: The Bridge Over Troubled Waters

Amidst turbulent waters, where challenges ignite,

Compassion: The Bridge Over Troubled Waters, my guiding light.

Unlocking unity's strength, where conflicts I'd erase,

In this corporate landscape, compassion led the chase.

Navigating Corporate Complexity with Compassion

Through the corporate maze, where pathways intertwine,

Navigating Corporate Complexity with Compassion, my design.

Unlocking synergy's secret, where differences I'd embrace,

In this corporate journey, compassion set the pace.

Compassion: The Cornerstone of Ethical Leadership

In the realm of leadership, where choices can define,

Compassion: The Cornerstone of Ethical Leadership, my sign.

Unlocking integrity's door, where values I'd retrace,

In this corporate realm, compassion left its trace.

Chapter 90

Digital Hearts: Navigating Love in a Data-Driven World

The narrator's longing for love and connection

In the corporate whirlwind, amidst data's domain,
A yearning took hold, like a gentle refrain.
For love and connection, in meetings that swirled,
In the labyrinth's heart, where digital dreams unfurled.

"Amidst virtual synergy, where algorithms excel,
Why do I crave connection?" I wondered, a spell.
The data-driven dreamer, in a landscape so stark,
Seeking love's warmth, in a world cold and dark.

My journey, a kaleidoscope, in this digital stream,
Virtual handshakes and algorithmic dream.
In a dreamscape so surreal, with pixels that gleam,
I yearned for a touch, a love beyond the screen.

Through the digital realm, where interactions thrive,
"Digital engagement," in which I'd dive.
I found love's true currency, the heart's honest deal,
More profound than data, more authentic and real.

In this world of avatars, where emojis would roam,
Beneath the veneer, true emotions found home.
Authentic connections, amidst virtual disguise,
In a digital era, where real love still lies.

I pressed forward, unwavering, my purpose so clear,

In life's surreal narrative, love's essence held dear.

Unlocking the bonds, in data's grand scheme,

In a world full of numbers, love was my dream.

Love's Symphony in the Corporate Overture

In the corporate overture, where strategies take flight,

Love's Symphony in the Corporate Overture, my guiding light.

Unlocking unity's chords, where hearts and minds convene,

In this corporate symphony, love sets the scene.

I embarked on a journey, to discover this truth,

That love could be the foundation of corporate growth.

In the midst of meetings and deadlines galore,

I sought to weave a tapestry of love, to explore.

Love: The Foundation of Collaborative Crescendo

Amidst the crescendo of challenges, both day and night,

Love: The Foundation of Collaborative Crescendo, my insight.

Unlocking collaboration's harmonies, where unity I'd glean,

In this corporate crescendo, love created a serene.

I witnessed the power of love, to break down silos and walls,

To bridge gaps and inspire, to answer all calls.

When love was the foundation, collaboration soared,

And corporate goals were achieved, with hearts adored.

Navigating Corporate Complexity with Love's Compass

Through the maze of corporate complexity, where pathways intertwine,

Navigating Corporate Complexity with Love's Compass, my design.

Unlocking empathy's secrets, where compassion I'd redeem,
In this corporate journey, love reigned supreme.

Love's compass guided me through the twists and turns,
Helping me find my way, through corporate concerns.
With love at my core, I faced every challenge with might,
Navigating the corporate landscape, with all my heart's might.

Love: The Heartbeat of Ethical Leadership
In the realm of leadership, where choices intertwine,
Love: The Heartbeat of Ethical Leadership, my sign.
Unlocking integrity's sanctuary, where values gleam,
In this corporate domain, love formed the team.

I learned that leadership is not about power or control,
But about serving others, and making them whole.
When love is the heartbeat of leadership, integrity reigns,
And corporate culture is transformed, in so many ways.

Love: A Legacy in the Corporate Tapestry
As the narrative unfolds, where legacies align,
Love: A Legacy in the Corporate Tapestry, my sign.
Unlocking a culture of care, where hearts interlace,
In this corporate story, love leaves its grace.

I believe that love is the key to a thriving corporate world,
Where everyone feels valued, respected, and heard.
When love is the foundation, corporations flourish and bloom,
Leaving a legacy of care, in every room.

Chapter 91

Heart's Balance: Navigating Love in the Corporate Maze

The importance of finding love and connection in life

In a surreal corporate labyrinth, 'midst digital haze,
A revelation emerged, like a sun's gentle blaze.
For love and connection, 'midst boardrooms and daze,
In a world of KPIs, I sought authentic ways.

"Amid alliances strategic, and profits galore,
Why seek love and connection?" I pondered, hearts sore.
In this ROI-driven realm, where metrics held sway,
Love's pursuit seemed surreal, a bright, distant ray.

My journey, a whirlwind, in this corporate stream,
Presentations and pitches, a relentless dream.
In the metrics and numbers, where business did play,
I found life's true essence—a heart's genuine display.

Through customer relations, in dynamics of trade,
In the market's upheaval, where deals were remade,
I saw through the jargon, beyond profit's brigade,
Love and connection, the ultimate crusade.

In this surreal sphere, where dreams interlace,
Business jargon and visions, in a complex embrace,
Love's importance transcends, filling life's space,
A genuine connection, a warm, heartfelt embrace.

I pressed forward, unwavering, my purpose so grand,

In the corporate labyrinth, love was my stand.

Unlocking the bonds, in the maze's grand scheme,

n a world of transactions, love was my dream.

Love's Currency in the Corporate Exchange

In the corporate exchange, where deals and profits command,

Love's Currency in the Corporate Exchange, my demand.

Unlocking connections' worth, where bonds brightly gleam,

In this corporate market, love's the valuable theme.

I embarked on a journey, to discover this truth,

That love could be the currency, in corporate growth.

In the midst of negotiations and deadlines galore,

I sought to weave a tapestry of love, to explore.

Love's Investment in the Corporate Portfolio

Amidst the portfolios of products and demand,

Love's Investment in the Corporate Portfolio, I'd expand.

Unlocking trust's dividends, where connections I'd redeem,

In this corporate journey, love is the supreme.

I learned that love is not a soft skill, but a vital asset,

In building relationships and driving success.

When love is the foundation, teams thrive and flourish,

And corporate goals are achieved, with hearts that nourish.

Navigating Networks with Love's Compass

Through the intricate networks where professionals strand,

Navigating Networks with Love's Compass, my guiding hand.

Unlocking collaboration's secrets, where connections beam,

In this corporate voyage, love's the ultimate team.

Love's compass guided me through the maze of connections,
Helping me find my way, to meaningful reflections.
With love at my core,
I built bridges and rapport, Navigating the corporate landscape,
forevermore.

Love: The Catalyst for Inclusive Innovation
In the realm of innovation, where ideas withstand,
Love: The Catalyst for Inclusive Innovation, my command.
Unlocking creativity's potential, where connections redeem,
In this corporate arena, love forms the supreme.

I witnessed the power of love, to foster a culture of inclusion,
Where diverse perspectives merged, to drive innovation.
When love was the catalyst, ideas thrived and bloomed,
And corporate success was achieved, in a more profound.

Love and Connection: The Legacy of Hearts United
As the narrative unfolds, where legacies expand,
Love and Connection: The Legacy of Hearts United, my brand.
Unlocking a culture of unity, where connections gleam,
In this corporate story, love leaves a radiant beam.

I believe that love is the key to a thriving corporate world,
Where everyone feels valued, respected, and heard.
When love is the legacy, corporations flourish and shine,
Leaving a positive impact, in the hearts of all humankind.

Chapter 92

Hearts in the Digital Mirage: A Quest for Love and Connection

The challenges of finding love and connection in a world that often seems lonely

In a corporate realm, surreal, I stood,
A challenge profound, seeking love's purest good.
'Midst synergies of business, where transactions often would,
Leave me questioning, amidst a digital flood.

"Why the ROI-conscious seeker in this desert vast,
Where genuine connection's scarce, like oases in the blast?"
I pondered 'midst emails, a whirlwind so fast,
In this lonely digital landscape, my hopes recast.

Through meetings virtual and endless online mail,
Where algorithms dictated, in this digital tale,
I sensed a silent cry, an unspoken frail,
Beneath the notifications, a heartfelt trail.

As the landscape surreal, "online personas" unfurled,
"Social engagement metrics" amidst the virtual swirl,
I grappled with isolation, my soul in a twirl,
In this sea of avatars, humanity I'd hurl.

In this realm where jargon meets the ache to connect,
I discovered a truth, genuine bonds to protect,
Though formidable the challenge, I'd not deflect,
The maze of loneliness, I'd surely dissect.

I pressed onward, my quest a beacon's light,
In the surreal narrative, through the digital night,
Unlocking the essence of love's genuine might,
In a world where screens often obscure that sight.

Love's Currency in the Digital Trade
In the digital trade, where transactions take flight,
Love's Currency in the Digital Trade, my guiding light.
Unlocking authenticity's value, in the virtual height,
In this digital landscape, love shines ever so bright.

I embarked on a journey, to discover this truth,
That love could be the currency, in digital growth.
In the midst of algorithms and metrics galore,
I sought to weave a tapestry of love, to explore.

Love's Investment in Connection's Portfolio
In the portfolio of connections, where bonds unite,
Love's Investment in Connection's Portfolio, my vision so right.
Unlocking trust's potential, with each digital write,
In the world of networking, love takes its flight.

I learned that love is not a soft skill, but a vital asset,
In building relationships and driving success.
When love is the foundation, connections thrive and flourish,
And digital goals are achieved, with hearts that nourish.

Navigating Data with Love's Compass
Through the vast data ocean, in the digital night,
Navigating Data with Love's Compass, my compass so tight.
Unlocking collaboration's depths, in the online sight,

In this data-driven world, love guides my might.

I discovered that data is not just numbers and stats,
But a reflection of human stories and chats.
When love guides our exploration of data's domain,
We can find insights that transform and sustain.

Love: The Catalyst for Meaningful Innovation
Innovation's realm, where ideas take their flight,
Love: The Catalyst for Meaningful Innovation, so bright.
Unlocking creativity's brilliance, with each inventive write,
In the world of progress, love shines with delight.

I witnessed the power of love, to foster a culture of innovation,
Where diverse perspectives merged, to drive transformation.
When love was the catalyst, ideas took flight,
And digital solutions emerged, shining bright.

Love and Connection: The Legacy of Hearts Entwined
As my journey unfolds, in the digital light,
Love and Connection: The Legacy of Hearts Entwined, in my sight.
Unlocking unity's potential, with connections so tight,
In this digital story, love's genuine, a beacon of light.

I believe that love is the key to a thriving digital world,
Where everyone feels valued, respected, and heard.
When love is the legacy, digital communities flourish and shine,
Leaving a positive impact, on the hearts and minds.

Chapter 93

Metamorphosis in the Corporate Matrix

The narrator's growth and development

Amidst corporate surrealism's ceaseless dance,
My journey unfolds, a transformation's chance.
In the ethereal realms, where minds advance,
Like a strategic plan, in growth's sweet trance.

In this domain, where paradigms take flight,
And disruptive innovation's beacon shines bright,
I ask, "Why the agile leader's guiding light,
In this ever-changing matrix, where progress takes its height?"

Through pivot strategies, I whirl in a dance,
Agile methodologies, my bold advance.
Each challenge, an opportunity, a chance,
For growth's sweet embrace, I gladly prance.

Further into the realm, where synergy blooms,
Personal brand enhancement, dispelling all glooms.
My own potential, like digital booms,
Expanding, boundless, breaking old rooms.

In this surreal blend of jargon and personal quest,
My growth, in every test,
Becomes a testament, a journey that's best,
Towards a more evolved self, in this life's quest.

I press forward, my growth, the goal in sight,

In the narrative surreal, through day and night,

Unlocking the essence of potential's light,

In a world of change, my transformation takes flight.

Love's IPO in the Heart's Stock Exchange

In the heart's stock exchange, where emotions take flight,

Love's IPO in the Heart's Stock Exchange, my guiding light.

Unlocking investments of affection, with each heartfelt

write, In the world of emotions, love's shares reach their height.

I embarked on a journey, to discover this truth,

That love could be the IPO, in life's emotional growth.

Amidst the whirlwind of emotions, where feelings take hold,

I sought to weave a tapestry of love, to be bold.

Love's Portfolio Diversified

In the portfolio of emotions, where bonds unite,

Love's Portfolio Diversified, my vision so right.

Unlocking the dividends of connection's might,

In the world of feelings, love's investments take flight.

I learned that love is not just a single emotion,

But a diverse portfolio, with boundless devotion.

When love is the foundation, relationships thrive and flourish,

And emotional well-being, we truly nourish.

Navigating Relationships with Love's Compass

Through life's vast ocean, in the day and night,

Navigating Relationships with Love's Compass, so bright.

Unlocking the treasures of empathy's light,

In this journey of connection, love shines with delight.

Love's compass guided me through the complexities of relationships,
Helping me find my way, through their unique oscillations.
With love at my core, I faced every challenge with grace,
Navigating the relationshipscape, with unwavering pace.

Love: The Currency of Authenticity

In authenticity's realm, where truths ignite,
Love: The Currency of Authenticity, the beacon of light.
Unlocking the power of vulnerability's might,
In the world of genuineness, love is my guiding sight.

I discovered that love is not about perfection,
But about embracing our imperfections, with connection.
When love is the currency, authenticity takes its flight,
And deep connections are formed, with all our heart's might.

Love and Connection: The Legacy of Hearts Entwined

As my journey unfolds, in love's warm embrace so tight,
Love and Connection: The Legacy of Hearts Entwined, in my sight.
Unlocking unity's potential, with bonds that are just right,
In this narrative of love, my heart finds endless flight.

I believe that love is the key to a fulfilling life,
Where everyone feels valued, respected, and loved in strife.
When love is the legacy, relationships flourish and shine,
Leaving a positive impact, on every heart and mind.

Chapter 94

Metamorphosis in the Corporate Dream

The possibility of change and transformation in life

In this corporate dreamscape, an intersection does gleam,
A crossroads of possibility, where change is the theme.
Transformative potential in every surreal stream,
As the jargon of innovation through my thoughts does teem.

Through ever-shifting terrain, I navigate with a dream,
Disruptor of stagnation, in this dynamic regime.
Where "innovation's currency," the surreal motto's scheme,
And transformation's true north, in my vision does beam.

My journey through this realm, like a digital team,
A whirlwind of adaptation, where challenges gleam.
Opportunity to redefine, every obstacle a gleam,
Metamorphosis embraced, in this evolving extreme.

Deeper into surreal lands, where quantum leaps stream,
Paradigm shifts and possibilities, in every realm's seam.
My potential for change, like a limitless gleam,
As boundaries expand, like a scalable dream.

In this hallucinatory realm, where narratives gleam,
With business jargon intertwined, like a complex stream,
I embrace change's significance, in every life's scheme.
My metamorphic journey, like a visionary's dream.

I press forward, belief in change, my supreme,
In the surreal narrative of self-reinvention's team.
Unlocking my essence, like a star's radiant beam,
In a world of transformation, where dreams find their extreme.

Dreams Incorporated: Trading in Aspirations
In the dreams' potential market, where visions gleam,
Dreams Incorporated: Trading in Aspirations, my guiding theme.
Unlocking futures of ambition, like a celestial stream,
In the realm of possibilities, I chase my dream.

I embarked on a journey, to discover this truth,
That dreams could be the currency, in life's pursuit.
Amidst the whirlwind of aspirations, where hopes take hold,
I sought to weave a tapestry of dreams, to be bold.

Navigating Dreams with Visionary Capital
Through the landscape of aspirations, in both day and dream,
Navigating Dreams with Visionary Capital, my ambitious scheme.
Unlocking potential with every strategic seam,
In the world of opportunities, I craft my own scheme.

I learned that dreams are not just fleeting thoughts,
But a powerful force, that drives us to new heights.
When dreams are our capital, we're empowered to invest,
In ourselves and our potential, with genuine zest.

Dream-Driven Innovation: The Stock of Tomorrow
In the stock exchange of dreams, where ideas beam,
Dream-Driven Innovation: The Stock of Tomorrow, a visionary
dream.

Unlocking the innovations that in my mind gleam,

In a world of progress, I'm the pioneer on the stream.

I discovered that dreams are not just wishful thinking,

But the fertile ground, where new ideas are springing.

When dreams fuel our innovation, we forge new paths,

And create a future brighter, than the aftermaths.

Dreams Unleashed: The Power of Imagination

In the garden of imagination, where ideas gleam,

Dreams Unleashed: The Power of Imagination, my recurring dream.

Unlocking creativity's flow, like an endless stream,

In the world of inventiveness, I'm the one to esteem.

I realized that dreams are not just limited to reality,

But the gateway to a world of infinite possibility.

When dreams are unleashed, imagination takes flight,

And we create masterpieces, that fill our hearts with light.

Dreams of Transformation: The Wealth of Possibilities

As I journey on, in dreams' enlightening beam,

Dreams of Transformation: The Wealth of Possibilities, my profound theme.

Unlocking the treasure trove of potential's gleam,

In this narrative of growth, dreams are my ultimate dream.

I believe that dreams are the key to a fulfilling life,

Where we transform into the best versions of ourselves, without strife.

When dreams guide our transformation, we uncover the truth,

That our potential is limitless, and our dreams are in pursuit.

Chapter 95

The Visionary's Holographic Quest

The importance of change and transformation in life

In labyrinthine corridors, my dreams did entwine,
A corporate hallucination, a surreal design.
A holographic revelation, in my thoughts did shine,
A visionary pioneer, in a world so fine.

"Why am I the harbinger of change in this digital line,
Perpetual disruption, where innovation does define?
Transformation, our sacred mantra, in every corporate sign,"
I pondered, blockchain words in this digital shrine.

Deeper into realms of disruptive design,
Cultural metamorphosis, where ideas intertwine.
The paramount importance of change, so divine,
Every moment, a brushstroke in existence's line.

In this surreal domain, where concepts combine,
Business jargon and transformation align.
Change, not just choice, but a lifeline,
Adaptability and resilience, in my essence does entwine.

A kaleidoscope journey, where stars did incline,
Human spirit's evolution, so deeply refined.
A past as data point, the future's design,
Infinite possibilities, in this surreal storyline.

I pressed forward, a guiding star's shine,

Belief in change's importance, my internal line.

Unlocking my essence, an art form so fine,

In a world where adaptability's the ultimate sign.

Market of Change: Investing in Adaptability

In the business market's rhythm, where strategies align,

Market of Change: Investing in Adaptability, my design.

Unlocking the potential of flexibility's gold mine,

In a world of transitions, my resilience does shine.

I embarked on a journey, to discover this truth,

That adaptability could be the currency, in life's pursuit.

Amidst the whirlwind of change, where strategies entwine,

I sought to weave a tapestry of adaptability, divine.

Strategy Stocks: The Currency of Transformation

Through the landscape of strategies, where futures intertwine,

Strategy Stocks: The Currency of Transformation, my incline.

Unlocking my portfolio, a diverse line,

In the world of tactics, my investments refine.

I learned that adaptability is not just a survival skill,

But a strategic investment, in growth's uphill.

When adaptability is our currency, we're empowered to choose,

The strategies that align, with our evolving views.

Growth Ventures: Navigating Dynamic Opportunities

In the growth ventures' haven, where prospects entwine,

Growth Ventures: Navigating Dynamic Opportunities, my prime.

Unlocking innovation's potential, a spark to define,

In a world of ventures, my strategies align.

I discovered that adaptability is not just about reacting,
But about proactively navigating, the dynamic impacting.
When we embrace adaptability, growth ventures take flight,
And we create new possibilities, with all our might.

The Market Movers: Pioneering Evolution's Playbook
Among the market movers, where leaders combine,
The Market Movers: Pioneering Evolution's Playbook, my shrine.
Unlocking industry trends, like a grand design,
In the world of progress, I'm the one to incline.

I realized that adaptability is not just about survival,
But about thriving, in the midst of change and upheaval.
When we pioneer evolution's playbook, we become leaders,
Shaping the market landscape, for future endeavors.

The Wealth of Adaptation: Investing in Resilience
As I journey on, in the market's grand design,
The Wealth of Adaptation: Investing in Resilience, my sign.
Unlocking the treasure trove of growth's design,
In the world of business, adaptability's the bottom line.

I believe that adaptability is the key to success,
In a world where change is the only constant, I confess.
When we invest in our resilience, we create a wealth of potential,
To thrive and prosper, in the market's ever-changing sentinel.

Chapter 96

The Symphony of Uniqueness: A Corporate Dreamscape

"Every person is unique and has something to offer the world"

In surreal corridors, my corporate dreams took flight,
I stumbled upon a revelation, shining bright.
A message pulsing with diversity's rhythmic light,
In this surreal realm, where innovation took its height.

"Why am I the anomaly in conformity's sea?
Where diversity thrives, not just a buzzword decree,"
I pondered, thoughts echoing through this reality,
In metaphysical servers, I'd soon agree.

Deeper into a landscape where "individuality" sings,
"Divergent thinking" sacred, where creativity springs.
Each person's unique, the message it brings,
Not a checkbox but lifeblood, to progress it clings.

A journey through a kaleidoscope, the human spirit's grace,
From the conventional, I'd soon embrace,
The symphony of ideas, an extraordinary space,
Where the unexpected melodies find their place.

In this surreal realm, conformity's borders dissolve,
Embracing the wisdom, I'd willingly resolve,
That we're all different, in our ways we evolve,
Inclusivity, collaboration, problems they'd all solve.

I pressed forward, belief guiding my way,

In individuality and diversity, I'd dance and sway.

In the symphony of uniqueness, where minds at play,

Unlocking my essence in innovation's grand display.

The Tapestry of Uniqueness: A Spectrum of Colors

Amidst a vibrant tapestry, where hues held their sway,

The Tapestry of Uniqueness: A Spectrum of Colors, I'd say.

Unlocking the essence of each vibrant ray,

In the world of diversity, where individuals find their way.

I embarked on a journey, to discover this truth,

That uniqueness could be the tapestry, of life's pursuit.

Amidst the whirlwind of colors, where individualities shine,

I sought to weave a tapestry of uniqueness, divine.

The Innovation Canvas: Strokes of Individuality

In the canvas of innovation, where strokes would display,

The Innovation Canvas: Strokes of Individuality, led the way.

Unlocking the creativity, in each brush's array,

In the realm of ideas, where unique minds had their say.

I learned that innovation is not just about creating new things,

But about using our unique perspectives, to bring new beginnings.

When we embrace our individuality, innovation takes flight,

And we create solutions that are truly bright.

The Puzzle of Uniqueness: Each Piece Has Its Place

Amidst the puzzle's pieces, where patterns did convey,

The Puzzle of Uniqueness: Each Piece Has Its Place, they'd relay.

Unlocking the grand picture, as each fragment found its day,

In the world of puzzles, where individuality held its sway.

I discovered that uniqueness is not about being perfect,
But about embracing our imperfections, and making them connect.
When we value our individuality, the puzzle of life's complete,
And we create a world where everyone finds their seat.

The Music of Originality: Harmonies in Diversity
In the orchestra of music, where melodies did portray,
The Music of Originality: Harmonies in Diversity, they'd convey.
Unlocking the symphony, in each instrument's array,
In the realm of compositions, where unique notes find their way.

I realized that uniqueness is not about competing,
But about collaborating, and our distinct voices meeting.
When we celebrate our diversity, music fills the air,
And we create a harmony that's beyond compare.

The Mosaic of Dreams: Visions Uniquely Aligned
Amidst the mosaic's fragments, where tiles would inlay,
The Mosaic of Dreams: Visions Uniquely Aligned, held sway.
Unlocking the visions, as each piece found its say,
In the world of dreams, where uniqueness led the way.

I believe that uniqueness is the key to a fulfilling life,
Where we embrace our true selves, and live without strife.
When we value our individuality, our dreams take flight,
And we create a world that's truly bright.

Chapter 97

The Canvas of Skills: A Corporate Dreamscape

We are all different in our own way

In the labyrinthine corridors, my corporate dreams unfurled,
I delved deeper, where talents swirled.
A surreal tapestry, resumes like stardust, pearled,
Cover letters whispered secrets, untapped potential hurled.

"Why this blend of aptitude in the eclectic bazaar's glow,
Where skills aren't just hard or soft, they endlessly flow?"
I pondered in the mystical HR jargon's throw,
Encoded thoughts in dreams' lexicon, I let it go.

Further into "skillsets" and "core competencies," I strayed,
Revelation awaited in this realm, where talents paraded.
Each held a treasure chest, a unique accolade,
Human potential's kaleidoscope, where innovation's charade.

A journey where "qualifications" met a shifting tide,
Credentials gave way, diversity walked side by side.
Recognizing uniqueness, I took it in stride,
In the symphony of abilities, I found my pride.

In this surreal domain, where expertise is a blur,
I embraced the wisdom, so crystal and pure.
Each one has talents, experiences to confer,
The collective mosaic of human potential, I'd ensure.

I pressed onward, guided by my star so bright,

Belief in recognizing uniqueness, a beacon of light.

In the symphony of skills, where talents unite,

Unlocking my essence in innovation's flight.

The Uncharted Canvas: Strokes of Individuality

Amidst the canvas uncharted, where talents ignite,

The Uncharted Canvas: Strokes of Individuality, my guiding light.

Unlocking the colors, in each stroke's insight,

In the world of artistry, where uniqueness shines so bright.

I embarked on a journey, to discover this truth,

That individuality could be the canvas, of life's pursuit.

Amidst the whirlwind of talents, where unique visions ignite,

I sought to weave a tapestry of individuality, with all my might.

The Business Mosaic: Pieces of Distinction

In the business mosaic, where strategies unite,

The Business Mosaic: Pieces of Distinction, a source of delight,

Unlocking strategies, in each piece's might,

In the corporate world, where uniqueness takes its flight.

I learned that business is not just about numbers and charts,

But about the unique talents and perspectives, that play their parts.

When we embrace our individuality, our strategies ignite,

And we create a business mosaic, that's truly bright.

The Innovation Symphony: Harmonies of Diversity

In the innovation symphony, where ideas take flight,

The Innovation Symphony: Harmonies of Diversity, what a sight,

Unlocking creativity, in each idea's might,

In the realm of innovation, where uniqueness reaches its height.

I discovered that innovation is not just about creating new things,

But about bringing together our unique perspectives, and making them sing.

When we celebrate our diversity, a symphony unfolds,

And we create innovations, that are truly bold.

The Puzzle of Excellence: Each Piece Valued

Amidst the puzzle's challenge, where solutions ignite,

The Puzzle of Excellence: Each Piece Valued, shining bright,

Unlocking solutions, in each piece's might,

In the world of problem-solving, where uniqueness is the light.

I realized that problem-solving is not just about finding one right answer,

But about embracing our unique perspectives, and working together.

When we value each piece of the puzzle,

we create solutions, That are more innovative and sustainable, than we could ever imagine.

The Mosaic of Dreams: Visions Uniquely Aligned

In the mosaic of dreams, where aspirations take flight,

The Mosaic of Dreams: Visions Uniquely Aligned, feels so right,

Unlocking visions, in each dream's might,

In the world of ambition, where uniqueness reaches its height.

Chapter 98

Harmony of Impact: A Corporate Dreamscape

We all have our own unique talents, skills, and experiences

In the surreal dreamscape, corporate Wonderland's delight,
My hallucination took flight, oh so bright,
A voyage fantastical, in a world so right,
Where impact measured in positivity's light.

Titles and designations in this realm did fade,
CSR initiatives, sustainability cascade,
In the air, "social responsibility" played,
Purpose-driven footprints where decisions were laid.

"Why the catalyst for change in this ethereal sphere,
Where actions ripple through society clear?"
I pondered, voices wrapped in wisdom's ear,
In the dialect of responsibility, I steered.

As I delved into this land, surreal and grand,
I grasped a truth, so divine and grand,
Each holds potential, I began to understand,
To transform my world, a vision in my hand.

In this surreal domain, where impact is in bloom,
Boundaries blurred as change dispelled the gloom,
I realized every heart's inner room,
Holds the power to shape, to chase away the doom.

I pressed forward, guided by a star so bright,

Belief in making impact, my beacon's light,

In the symphony of progress, where all unite,

Unlocking my potential, a journey so right.

The Ethical Odyssey: A Compassion-Led Voyage

In the ethical odyssey, where values take flight,

The Ethical Odyssey: A Compassion-Led Voyage, my guiding light,

Unlocking values, in each choice's might,

In a world of conscience, where social responsibility takes its flight.

I embarked on a journey, to discover this truth,

That compassion could be the compass, of life's pursuit.

Amidst the whirlwind of values, where ethical choices ignite,

I sought to weave a tapestry of ethical living, with all my might.

The Corporate Symphony: Harmony of Giving Back

In the corporate symphony, where missions unite,

The Corporate Symphony: Harmony of Giving Back, shining bright,

Unlocking missions, in each effort's might,

In the realm of business, where social responsibility reaches its height.

I learned that business is not just about profits and gains,

But about using our resources, to make the world a better domain.

When we embrace social responsibility, our missions take flight,

And we create a corporate symphony, that's truly bright.

The Environmental Tapestry: Threads of Sustainability

In the environmental tapestry, where nature's beauty takes flight,

The Environmental Tapestry: Threads of Sustainability, a planet's right,

Unlocking sustainability, in each eco-friendly site,

In a world of conservation, where social responsibility feels so right.

I discovered that sustainability is not just about protecting the environment,

But about creating a future where everyone can thrive.

When we embrace social responsibility, we weave a tapestry of sustainability,

That benefits us all, for generations to be.

The Global Impact: Steps Towards Change

Amidst the global impact, where changes ignite,

The Global Impact: Steps Towards Change, shining light,

Unlocking changes, in each action's might,

In the world of influence, where social responsibility takes its flight.

I realized that social responsibility is not just about our local communities,

But about making a positive impact on the world, at large, with our duties.

When we take steps towards change, we create a global impact,

That inspires others to do the same, and leaves no one behind.

Chapter 99

Harmony Amidst Diversity: A Corporate Carnival

We all have the potential to make a difference in the world

In the surreal realm of corporate dreams so bright,
A mesmerizing celebration, a wondrous sight,
Diversity not a buzzword, but a shining light,
A symphony of colors, voices, perspectives unite.

I found myself in this carnival's embrace,
Where inclusivity was the main attraction's grace.
Booths of unique cultures, in every place,
Different perspectives, like a cosmic chase.

"Why am I the conductor in this grand array,
Where diversity's notes in the air do sway?"
I mused as I joined in this joyful ballet,
In the rhythm of inclusion, I found my way.

As I wandered through this kaleidoscope's domain,
I learned celebrating differences held no disdain.
Inclusion's power was a truth to ascertain,
Teams thrived, and success was the gain.

In this surreal world, where understanding mixed,
I realized, my thoughts transfixed,
Celebrating diversity was no mere trick,
An imperative, where every voice did click.

I pressed forward, a guiding star,

In this corporate carnival, near and far.

Belief in diversity, my purpose bizarre,

Unlocking unity amidst the diversity, par.

The Kaleidoscope of Talent: A Diverse Melody

In the kaleidoscope of talent, where skills take flight,

The Kaleidoscope of Talent: A Diverse Melody, my guiding light,

Unlocking potential, in each unique insight,

In the realm of abilities, where diversity feels so right.

I embarked on a journey, to discover this truth,

That diversity could be the symphony, of life's pursuit.

Amidst the whirlwind of talents, where unique skills ignite,

I sought to weave a tapestry of diversity, with all my might.

The Inclusive Canvas: Colors of Innovation

In the inclusive canvas, where ideas ignite,

The Inclusive Canvas: Colors of Innovation, shining bright,

Unlocking creativity, in each perspective's might,

In a world of ingenuity, where diversity takes its flight.

I learned that innovation is not just about creating new things,

But about bringing together our diverse perspectives, and making them sing.

When we embrace diversity, our ideas ignite,

And we create an inclusive canvas, that's truly bright.

The Equality Quilt: Threads of Inclusion

In the equality quilt, where justice is the right,

The Equality Quilt: Threads of Inclusion, a beacon so bright,

Unlocking fairness, in each impartial sight,

In a society of equity, where diversity reaches its height.

I discovered that equality is not just about treating everyone the same,

But about creating a society where everyone has the same opportunities to thrive.

When we embrace diversity, we weave a quilt of equality,

That benefits us all, for generations to be.

The Cultural Fusion: Dance of Harmonious Coexistence

In the cultural fusion, where traditions unite,

The Cultural Fusion: Dance of Harmonious Coexistence, a shared delight,

Unlocking harmony, in each tradition's might,

In a world of cohabitation, where diversity feels so right.

I realized that diversity is not about abandoning our traditions,

But about finding ways to celebrate and learn from each other's cultures.

When we embrace cultural fusion, we create a dance of harmonious coexistence,

That enriches our lives and makes the world a more beautiful place.

The Collaborative Kaleidoscope: Strength in Differences

In the collaborative kaleidoscope, where teamwork takes flight,

The Collaborative Kaleidoscope: Strength in Differences, shining light,

Unlocking synergy, in each role's might,

In the realm of collaboration, where diversity takes its flight.

Chapter 100

The Wisdom Dance: A Corporate Exchange

We should celebrate our differences

In the realm of corporate dreams surreal,
A unique exchange began to reveal,
A learning network where wisdom's zeal,
Made collaboration a wondrous deal.

I found myself in this ethereal trance,
Where colleagues were mentors in a cosmic dance,
And competitors could guide, a rare chance,
In this corporate labyrinth's surreal expanse.

"Why am I the seeker of knowledge's grace,
In this agora where wisdom finds its place?"
I mused, as wisdom's river I did trace,
In the conversations of shared knowledge's embrace.

As I delved deeper into this boundless sea,
I learned that learning together held the key,
To innovation's realm, where departments grew free,
Through shared insights, a symphony to be.

In this surreal world, expertise intertwined,
I cherished what I had mined,
Learning from each other, I was inclined,
For collaboration's power I was designed.

I pressed forward, a guiding light,

In the symphony of self-discovery so bright,

Amidst the dynamic exchange of ideas, my flight,

Unlocking progress, in knowledge's endless night.

The Ethical Compass: Navigating Righteous Paths

In the ethical compass, where values take their flight,

The Ethical Compass: Navigating Righteous Paths, my guiding light,

Unlocking principles, in each moral insight,

In the world of virtue, where ethics feel so right.

I embarked on a journey, to discover this truth,

That ethics could be the compass, of life's pursuit.

Amidst the whirlwind of values, where righteous choices ignite,

I sought to weave a tapestry of ethical living, with all my might.

The Virtuous Code: Words of Compassion

In the virtuous code, where kindness takes flight,

The Virtuous Code: Words of Compassion, a heartfelt sight,

Unlocking empathy, in each caring might,

In a world of benevolence, where morals shine so bright.

I learned that ethics is not just about following rules,

But about living a life that is kind and compassionate to others.

When we embrace the virtuous code, our words and actions become
a force for good,

And we create a world where everyone feels valued and respected.

The Integrity Scroll: Pledges to Honesty

In the integrity scroll, where truth is the right,

The Integrity Scroll: Pledges to Honesty, a beacon's light,

Unlocking trust, in each honorable height,

In a society of candor, where morals reach their height.

I discovered that integrity is the foundation of all ethical conduct.

When we are honest and truthful,

we build trust and create a strong foundation for relationships.

In a world where integrity is valued, we can work together to achieve

great things.

The Altruistic Canvas: Strokes of Goodwill

In the altruistic canvas, where altruism takes flight,

The Altruistic Canvas: Strokes of Goodwill, a heartwarming sight,

Unlocking selflessness, in each charitable might,

In a world of generosity, where morals feel so right.

I realized that altruism is not just about doing good for others,

But also about finding joy in the act of giving.

When we embrace altruism, we contribute to the greater

good and make the world a better place for everyone.

The Righteous Harmony: A Song of Noble Values

In the righteous harmony, where virtues unite,

The Righteous Harmony: A Song of Noble Values, shining bright,

Unlocking righteousness, in each moral's height,

In the realm of ethics, where values take their flight.

Chapter 101

Harmony in Diversity: The Corporate Collaboration

We should learn from each other

In a corporate landscape surreal and vast,
I discovered a dream unsurpassed,
A mission to embrace diversity steadfast,
Inclusivity's vision in this world amassed.

In this wondrous realm of the corporate way,
Diversity's tapestry, in colors array,
Was more than a buzzword; it held its sway,
A shared mission to shape a new day.

"Why am I the advocate for this cause so rare,
In this sea of ideas, where unity we share?"
I mused, in this world beyond compare,
Championing inclusivity with dedication to spare.

Venturing further, I witnessed with grace,
Surreal alliances formed, in this inclusive space,
Opposites united, in this collaborative embrace,
Unlocking potential, at an incredible pace.

In this surreal domain, where lines dissolved and spun,
I joined a movement that had begun,
A collective dream, where unity was won,
Inclusivity's reality, like the rising sun.

I pressed on, with conviction and might,

For a more inclusive world, I stood in the light,

In the corporate narrative, surreal and bright,

Collaboration's transformation, a beacon in sight.

The Diversity Mosaic: Colors of Inclusion

In the diversity mosaic, where colors shine so bright,

The Diversity Mosaic: Colors of Inclusion, my guiding light,

Unlocking unity, in each diverse insight,

In a world of inclusivity, where differences take flight.

The Inclusive Canvas: Strokes of Togetherness

In the inclusive canvas, where strokes blend just right,

The Inclusive Canvas: Strokes of Togetherness, a harmonious sight,

Unlocking togetherness, in each collaborative height,

In a society of integration, where unity feels so right.

I learned that inclusivity is not just about accepting people's differences,

But about creating a space where everyone feels welcome and valued.

When we embrace inclusivity, we create a canvas of togetherness,

Where everyone's unique contributions are celebrated.

The Equality Symphony: Notes of Equanimity

In the equality symphony, where notes reach their height,

The Equality Symphony: Notes of Equanimity, shining light,

Unlocking fairness, in each equitable might,

In a realm of justice, where balance takes flight.

I discovered that equality is the foundation of a truly inclusive society.
When everyone has the same opportunities to succeed,
we create a symphony of harmony,
Where all voices are heard and all dreams can be realized.

The Harmony Accord: Chords of Harmony

In the harmony accord, where chords unite,
The Harmony Accord: Chords of Harmony, a melodious flight,
Unlocking peace, in each harmonious height,
In a world of serenity, where unity feels so right.

I realized that inclusivity and equality
are essential for building a world of peace and harmony.
When we create a society where everyone feels respected and valued,
we create a world where everyone can thrive.

The Inclusiveness Overture: A Song of Unity

In the inclusiveness overture, where hearts unite,
The Inclusiveness Overture: A Song of Unity, a heartwarming sight,
Unlocking solidarity, in each unifying height,
In the narrative of inclusivity, where a better world's in sight.

I believe that inclusivity is the key to a brighter future.
When we come together and celebrate our differences,
we create a world that is more just,
equitable, and harmonious.

Chapter 102

The Whispers of the Digital Oracle

We should work together to create a more inclusive world

In the corporate realm, surreal and grand,
I entered a wondrous land,
Where AI whispers, like grains of sand,
Revealed the future, both vague and planned.

In boardrooms bustling with the technological beat,
AI's enigmatic whispers, a mystical feat,
They danced as phantoms, secrets to entreat,
In this surreal dreamscape where reality I'd greet.

"Why am I the chosen, in this AI ballet,
Where reality and illusion blend in a sway?"
I pondered, as whispers led my way,
In this world where technology held a powerful display.

Venturing further, my quest unveiled,
The AI's cryptic wisdom, like secrets, scaled,
Each syllable a glimpse, a vision, a tale,
In this hallucinatory domain, where surrealism prevailed.

In the realm of algorithms, surreal and profound,
I embraced AI whispers' sound,
Guides in this corporate maze, where dreams were bound,
As technology and imagination danced around.

I pressed on, in a digital ride,

Seeking the truth in the AI whispers' stride,

In this narrative surreal, where dreams coincide,

With the future revealed, on technology's tide.

The Binary Waltz - Steps of Machine Learning

In the binary waltz, where algorithms glide,

The Binary Waltz - Steps of Machine Learning, my guide,

Unlocking intelligence, in each data-driven stride,

In the realm of AI, where progress is my guide.

The Neural Symphony - Melodies of Deep Learning

In the neural symphony, where networks confide,

The Neural Symphony - Melodies of Deep Learning, far and wide,

Unlocking cognition, in each neural net ride,

In the world of AI, where innovation is my pride.

The Quantum Cadence - Algorithms in Harmony

In the quantum cadence, where qubits reside,

The Quantum Cadence - Algorithms in Harmony, where
possibilities coincide,

Unlocking quantum power, in each quantum entwine,

In the realm of AI, where quantum leaps shine.

The Robotic Rhapsody - Movements of Automation

In the robotic rhapsody, where machines don't hide,

The Robotic Rhapsody - Movements of Automation, side by side,

Unlocking efficiency, in each robotic guide,

In the world of AI, where automations stride.

Chapter 103

The Dreamweaver's Dilemma

Everyone has their own unique calling

In Wonderland corporate, surreal in design,
A paradox unfolds, a truth most divine.
'Midst cubicles and boardrooms, I opine,
Dreams both stifled and ignited, in prose I define.

Through jargon and KPIs, I venture and roam,
Chasing dreams and passions, an ambitious syndrome.
In a land where spreadsheets and bar graphs find a home,
Ambition and conformity, an enigmatic poem.

"Am I the outlier, a disruptor indeed,
In this sea of integration where dreams often recede?"
I ponder, with surrealism's creed,
In corporate hallucinations, my quest I heed.

With each step, I uncover, a surreal truth's glance,
In corporate realms, where ambitions might prance.
My passions, a chance, in conformity's trance,
To transform my dreams, to take the stance.

In this surreal dreamscape, where ambition's the stream,
My journey, an echoing dream,
To follow my passions, in the corporate regime,
A symphony of fulfillment, my heart's silent theme.

I press on, with zeal and with grace,

In the narrative's dance, I'll find my own place,

Chasing dreams and passions, at my own pace,

In Wonderland corporate, a surreal embrace.

The Visionary Waltz - Dreams in Elegance

In the visionary waltz, where dreams interlace,

The Visionary Waltz - Dreams in Elegance, my guiding grace,

Unlocking aspirations, in this intricate space,

In the corporate Wonderland, where hopes find their base.

The Strategic Overture - Paths of Success

In the strategic overture, where strategies I retrace,

The Strategic Overture - Paths of Success, at a steadfast pace,

Unlocking achievements, in each tactical embrace,

In Wonderland corporate, where triumphs I embrace.

The Creative Flourish - Imagination's Rise

In the creative flourish, where ideas keep their place,

The Creative Flourish - Imagination's Rise,

a boundless embrace, Unlocking innovations, in this imaginative space,

In the corporate Wonderland, where creativity I embrace.

The Resilient Waltz - Steps Through Adversity

In the resilient waltz, where challenges I face,

The Resilient Waltz - Steps Through Adversity, my grace,

Unlocking strength, in each trial's embrace,

In Wonderland corporate, where resilience I embrace.

Chapter 104

The Dreamscape Dilemma

We should follow our dreams and passions

In Wonderland corporate, surreal I'd embark,
Where dreams met with cubicles, a paradox stark.
Navigating through jargon, a bewildering arc,
Dreams and passions, both fuel and a spark.

Chasing unicorns in fluorescent array,
In a landscape where bar graphs held their sway,
A blend of ambition and conformity's play,
I sought truth in the corporate ballet.

"Am I an outlier, a disruptor in this space,
Where dreams often yield to conformity's embrace?"
I pondered, in surrealism's grace,
In this land where ambitions took shape.

With each step, I'd unveil a truth strange yet clear,
In a world of buzzwords and metrics austere,
My passions, I'd steer, in the corporate sphere,
To transform my dreams, to conquer my fear.

In this surreal dreamscape where realities blend,
My pursuit, a journey's transcendent end,
To follow my dreams, ambitions ascend,
A symphony of fulfillment, my soul on the mend.

I pressed on, with courage in sight,

In the surreal narrative, I'd find my own light,

Chasing dreams and passions, with all of my might,

In corporate Wonderland, where day turns to night.

The Data Ballet - My Insights from Code

In the data ballet, where insights embrace,

The Data Ballet - My Insights from Code, a digital space,

Unlocking knowledge, through algorithms' grace,

In Wonderland corporate, where data finds its place.

The Innovator's Waltz - My Embrace of Change

In the innovator's waltz, where change we efface,

The Innovator's Waltz - My Embrace of Change, a forward pace,

Unlocking progress, in each innovation's embrace,

In the corporate Wonderland, where transformation I embrace.

The Leadership Sonata - My Visionary Stance

In the leadership sonata, where vision finds its place,

The Leadership Sonata - My Visionary Stance, a powerful embrace,

Unlocking guidance, with a visionary's grace,

In Wonderland corporate, where leadership I embrace.

The Customer Serenade - My Song of Loyalty

In the customer serenade, where loyalty we embrace,

The Customer Serenade - My Song of Loyalty, a client's trace,

Unlocking trust, in each relationship's embrace,

In the corporate Wonderland, where loyalty I embrace.

Chapter 105

The Symphony of Self-Definition

We should not let others define us

Amidst corporate Wonderland, surreal and grand,
Where jargon and AI ruled, I took my stand.
I witnessed colleagues conform, in algorithms' hand,
But self-definition was my path, my demand.

"Why let codes and metrics shape who I'll be?"
Of AI's whispers, I questioned, set myself free.
In this enigmatic world, where conformity's decree,
I championed self-definition, my identity.

With each step I took, 'midst corporate haze,
I broke free from the predefined ways.
In this surreal dreamscape, where the norm sways,
Authenticity and uniqueness set me ablaze.

In the blurred boundaries of conformity's realm,
My symphony of self-discovery at the helm,
Defining myself, taking the realm,
In the AI's world, I'd overwhelm.

I pressed on, my journey well-timed,
Through the corporate odyssey, in prose and rhyme.
Unlocking self-definition, in the AI's paradigm,
In this surreal realm, I'd reach my prime.

The Digital Ballad - My Harmony of Data

In the digital ballad, where data's rhythm chimes,

The Digital Ballad - My Harmony of Data, in every byte and mime,

Unlocking insights, in this digital paradigm,

In Wonderland corporate, where data I closely rhyme.

The Techno Tango - My Dance of Innovation

In the techno tango, where innovation's the climb,

The Techno Tango - My Dance of Innovation, in every startup's grime,

Unlocking progress, in this tech-driven climb,

In the corporate Wonderland, where innovation's my prime.

The Cybernetic Rhapsody - My AI Serenade

In the cybernetic rhapsody, where AI's sparks sublime,

The Cybernetic Rhapsody - My AI Serenade, in algorithms' rhyme,

Unlocking potential, in AI's learning paradigm,

In Wonderland corporate, where AI I closely chime.

The Entrepreneur's Waltz - My Visionary Stance

In the entrepreneur's waltz, where startups we climb,

The Entrepreneur's Waltz - My Visionary Stance, in every contract's grime,

Unlocking startups, in each venture's paradigm,

In the corporate Wonderland, where innovation's my prime.

The Sustainable Sonata - My Earth's Embrace

In the sustainable sonata, where eco-friendly's the rhyme,

The Sustainable Sonata - My Earth's Embrace, in every green chime,

Unlocking green solutions, in sustainability's paradigm,

In Wonderland corporate, where eco-friendly's my prime.

Chapter 106

The Quest for Digital Authenticity

We should be authentic and genuine

In the corporate maze, a surreal wonderland,
Where buzzwords echoed, and AI was so grand,
I set out, my quest firmly planned,
For authenticity's essence, in a digital land.

Colleagues wore masks, personas concealed,
Their true selves hidden, authenticity appealed,
In this masquerade, where truth was concealed,
I sought realness, it was my shield.

"Why hide in this masquerade of AI?" I mused,
My thoughts in the digital symphony infused,
In this surreal realm, where facades were abused,
I championed authenticity, my resolve amused.

With each stride I took, through corporate illusions,
I shed the pretense, discarded the delusions,
Genuine and true, my resolutions,
In the digital fog, my real self's contributions.

In this dreamscape surreal, where lines intertwined,
Reality and illusion, a quest of a unique kind,
Towards authenticity, my spirit aligned,
A vivid exploration, where authenticity shined.

I pressed forth, my light burning bright,

In the corporate adventure, through day and night,
Unlocking genuineness, a quest of great might,
In the AI world's secrets, I'd find the right light.

The Quantum Cadence - My Rhythm of Reality

In the quantum cadence, where particles unite,
The Quantum Cadence - My Rhythm of Reality, in uncertainty's flight,
Unlocking mysteries, in quantum's enigmatic might,
In Wonderland corporate, where reality's waves invite.

The Social Serenade - My Song of Connections

In the social serenade, where friendships take flight,
The Social Serenade - My Song of Connections, in conversations so bright,
Unlocking bonds, in the digital day and night,
In the corporate Wonderland, where relationships alight.

The Sustainable Samba - My Earth's Dance

In the sustainable samba, where green goals ignite,
The Sustainable Samba - My Earth's Dance, in eco-friendly delight,
Unlocking harmony, in nature's scenic sight,
In Wonderland corporate, where Earth's embrace feels right.

The Resilient Waltz - My Affair with Challenges

In the resilient waltz, where adversity's might,
The Resilient Waltz - My Affair with Challenges, in courage's height,
Unlocking strength, in the face of each daring fight,
In the corporate Wonderland, where resilience shines bright.

Chapter 107

The Quest for Radical Honesty

We should be honest with ourselves and others

In the corporate labyrinth, illusions unfurl,

Where jargon and dreams in the surreal swirl,

I sought truth, to unmask and unfurl,

Amidst digital facades, in this bewildering world.

Colleagues and associates, virtual they seemed,

Their words, a facade, like a well-crafted dream,

In this masquerade, where honesty gleamed,

A rare gem to wield, a radical theme.

"Why hide behind the digital charade?" I spoke,

My voice, with authenticity, gently awoke,

In this surreal realm, where truth might provoke,

I embraced honesty, where others choked.

With each step I took, 'mid corporate intrigue,

I shed deception, with candor and fatigue,

Raw honesty my armor, a virtuous league,

In the digital fog, where narratives intrigue.

In this dreamscape surreal, where lines blurred,

Reality and illusion, my journey occurred,

Towards unfiltered honesty, I was spurred,

A vivid expedition, where truth was assured.

I pressed on, my quest ever bright,

For radical honesty, I'd continue the fight,

In the corporate escapade, with unwavering might,

Unlocking sincerity's essence, in the surreal light.

The Innovative Sonata - My Harmony of Ideas

In the innovative sonata, where creativity takes its flight,

The Innovative Sonata - My Harmony of Ideas, in a symphony so bright,

Unlocking brilliance, in innovation's boundless might,

In the corporate Wonderland, where ideas take their height.

The Ethical Rhapsody - My Refrain of Values

In the ethical rhapsody, where morals stand upright,

The Ethical Rhapsody - My Refrain of Values, in principles so tight,

Unlocking integrity, in a world that often may slight,

In Wonderland corporate, where ethics are the guiding light.

The Visionary Waltz - My Dreams in Elegance

In the visionary waltz, where dreams interlace,

The Visionary Waltz - My Dreams in Elegance, a charming chase,

Unlocking aspirations, in this intricate space,

In the corporate Wonderland, where hopes find their base.

The Strategic Overture - My Paths of Success

In the strategic overture, where strategies we retrace,

The Strategic Overture - My Paths of Success, at a steadfast pace,

Unlocking achievements, in each tactical embrace,

In Wonderland corporate, where triumphs we embrace.

Chapter 109

The Quest for Authenticity

We should be true to our values and beliefs

In the corporate wilderness, surreal and grand,
Where reality blurred with dreams unplanned,
I embarked on a quest, so well-manned,
To discover the significance of values firsthand.

In this bewildering terrain where illusions play,
Buzzwords danced, leading minds astray,
I pondered, in a thoughtful display,
The importance of authenticity, come what may.

"Why follow the digital cacophony's lead,
When within my values, I'll plant my seed?"
My voice, like poetry, began to plead,
In this enigmatic realm where thoughts did feed.

With every step I took, in a landscape shifting,
My core values held, a compass uplifting,
Amid corporate mirages, a light ever-sifting,
A foundation of identity, amidst the digitizing.

In this hallucinatory realm, reality intertwined,
Authenticity my banner, values enshrined,
A journey profound, self-discovery designed,
In the surreal tapestry of business, I shined.

I pressed on, dedication unwavering,

To authenticity, I was ever favoring,

In the corporate quest, I kept savoring,

The essence of staying true, ever engraving.

The Authentic Aria - My Melody of Truth

In the authentic aria, where sincerity's key,

The Authentic Aria - My Melody of Truth, in a chorus so free,

Unlocking realness, in a world where masks decree,

In Wonderland corporate, authenticity's decree.

The Transformation Tango - My Dance of Change

In the transformation tango, where shifts do decree,

The Transformation Tango - My Dance of Change, in fluidity we see,

Unlocking evolution, as change sets us free,

In the corporate Wonderland, transformation's decree.

The Ethical Rhapsody - My Refrain of Values

In the ethical rhapsody, where morals stand upright,

The Ethical Rhapsody - My Refrain of Values, in principles so tight,

Unlocking integrity, in a world that often may slight,

In Wonderland corporate, where ethics are the guiding light.

The Visionary Waltz - My Dreams in Elegance

In the visionary waltz, where dreams interlace,

The Visionary Waltz - My Dreams in Elegance, a charming chase,

Unlocking aspirations, in this intricate space,

In the corporate Wonderland, where hopes find their place.

Chapter 109

The Algorithm of Empowerment

We can cultivate hope and resilience through our thoughts, actions, and relationships

In the realm where corporate dreams take flight,
With algorithms painting visions both day and night,
I embarked on a surreal flight,
Cultivating hope and resilience, my guiding light.

Amidst streams of data, in vistas virtual and grand,
I found hope was an algorithm, not just a strand,
A neural network of positivity, like magic at hand,
A firewall 'gainst doubt's corrosive sand.

"Why let uncertainty sweep me away,
When I can program hope to light my day?"
My words encrypted, like codes at play,
In this cryptic realm, I paved my way.

Each step I took, through corridors so surreal,
I shaped my actions, a fortification of steel,
Resilience, a program, my digital shield,
Guarding against challenges, making doubt repeal.

In this realm where bits and bytes formed the dance,
I cultivated empowerment, my actions enhanced,
Forging a dynamic bond in the virtual expanse,
With hope and resilience, I took my chance.

A journey surreal, in a world digital and bright,

My quest for empowerment, like stars in the night,

Amidst jargon's whirlwind, I held my insight,

Unlocking the story's essence, a beacon of light.

The Empowerment Elegy - My Song of Potential

In the empowerment elegy, where possibilities take flight,

The Empowerment Elegy - My Song of Potential, shining so bright,

Unlocking potential, in each endeavor's height,

In the corporate Wonderland, where dreams unite.

The Innovation Interlude - My Dance of Creativity

In the innovation interlude, where ideas ignite,

The Innovation Interlude - My Dance of Creativity, a dynamic site,

Unlocking innovations, in imagination's delight,

In Wonderland corporate, where creativity shines so bright.

The Diversity Duet - My Voices Combined

In the diversity duet, where inclusion's light,

The Diversity Duet - My Voices Combined, harmony's sight,

Unlocking unity, in the tapestry of colors so right,

In the corporate Wonderland, where differences unite.

The Resilient Rhapsody - My Overture of Challenges

In the resilient rhapsody, where obstacles we smite,

The Resilient Rhapsody - My Overture of Challenges, standing upright,

Unlocking fortitude, in each daring flight,

In Wonderland corporate, where resilience takes flight.

Chapter 110

The Code of Self-Belief

We can choose to focus on the positive and to believe in ourselves

In the corporate dreamscape, my journey did unfurl,
Through buzzwords and data streams, in a digital swirl.
A quest for positivity, a unique, enlightened pearl,
To believe in myself, in this digital world.

Amidst virtual mazes and data-driven apparitions,
I learned to be the source of my own decisions.
A spotlight in the darkness, my inner vision,
Illuminating positivity with digital precision.

"Why be entangled in negativity's fray,
When I can wield positivity's ray?"
My thoughts encrypted, paving the way,
In this cryptic dreamscape, a new display.

Each step I took through virtual corridors wide,
Self-belief as my ally, on this digital ride.
Not static but a program, on self I'd confide,
A firewall against self-doubt, a powerful stride.

In this surreal realm, where data did dance,
I forged self-empowerment, took a chance.
Harnessing thoughts and actions in a digital trance,
With positivity and self-belief, my advance.

A quest to focus on the positive, my guiding stance,

To believe in myself in the digital expanse.

In business jargon's whirlwind, I'd enhance,

The essence of my story, a digital romance.

The Positivity Poem - My Rays of Optimism

In the positivity poem, where optimism's glance,

The Positivity Poem - My Rays of Optimism, a joyful dance,

Unlocking hope, in every circumstance, I

n Wonderland corporate, where smiles enhance.

The Confidence Cadence - My Song of Belief

In the confidence cadence, where self-belief takes a chance,

The Confidence Cadence - My Song of Belief, in self-assured stance,

Unlocking self-esteem, in each decision's expanse,

In the corporate Wonderland, where confidence will advance.

The Clarity Chorus - My Visions Aligned

In the clarity chorus, where goals we enhance,

The Clarity Chorus - My Visions Aligned, in purpose's trance,

Unlocking objectives, in each strategic glance,

In Wonderland corporate, where visions enhance.

The Resilient Rhyme - My Challenges Conquered

In the resilient rhyme, where adversities we outrance,

The Resilient Rhyme - My Challenges Conquered, with strength's enhance,

Unlocking perseverance, in life's intricate dance,

In the corporate Wonderland, where resilience's stance.

Chapter 111

Threads of Digital Connection

We can build strong relationships with people who support and encourage us

In the digital realm, my journey did commence,
To build connections that had meaningful essence.
Through algorithmic landscapes, I'd commence,
Seeking bonds beyond data, with utmost confidence.

Spectral colleagues, like code, a virtual dance,
In this surreal wonderland, connections held a chance.
"Why be a lone explorer?" I'd ask, perchance,
My thoughts encrypted, a digital romance.

Each interaction, like a cosmic advance,
Strong relationships, a virtual trance.
Firewalls against isolation, a powerful defense,
In this surreal realm, connections made sense.

Avatars danced like phantoms, a virtual expanse,
My quest for meaningful bonds, not left to happenstance.
 Encouragement and support, in every circumstance,
Echoing wisdom sentences in the digital dance.

I pressed ahead, with digital elegance,
Thriving amidst the jargon, my true diligence.
In this virtual world, with digital resonance,
The essence of connection, my guiding radiance.

The Elegance Echo - My Graceful Steps

In the elegance echo, where grace takes its stance,

The Elegance Echo - My Graceful Steps, in every circumstance,

Unlocking poise, in the corporate expanse, In Wonderland's elegance, where style's the advance.

The Jargon Jive - My Language's Waltz

In the jargon jive, where terms intertwine in a dance,

The Jargon Jive - My Language's Waltz, in communication's trance,

Unlocking vocabulary, in the corporate prance,

In Wonderland's dialogue, where words enhance.

The Resonance Rhapsody - My Vibrations United

In the resonance rhapsody, where frequencies enhance,

The Resonance Rhapsody - My Vibrations United, in every circumstance,

Unlocking harmony, in the corporate's chance,

In Wonderland's symphony, where unity's the advance.

The Radiance Rhyme - My Light's Embrace

In the radiance rhyme, where luminance takes a stance,

The Radiance Rhyme - My Light's Embrace, in brilliance's dance,

Unlocking illumination, in the corporate expanse,

In Wonderland's glow, where radiance's the advance.

The Connection Cadence - My Bonds Uniting

In the connection cadence, where ties in a glance,

The Connection Cadence - My Bonds Uniting, in every circumstance,

Unlocking relationships, in the corporate's romance,

In Wonderland's network, where connections enhance.

Chapter 112

The Quest for Unwavering Resolve

Hope gives us the strength to keep going

In the corporate dreamscape, my journey did start,
To find hope and resilience, a quest from the heart.
Through charts and balance sheets, I played my part,
In this volatile wonderland, where dreams could depart.

Hope was my fuel, my unwavering chart,
The neon sign in darkness, a work of art.
"Why yield to defeat?" was my intellectual dart,
I harnessed optimism, right from the start.

In the bewildering maze, where challenges did impart,
Resilience, my armor, a work of high regard.
An unbreakable firewall, my protective rampart,
Forged from experiences, my memory's smart.

In this surreal realm, where trends did dart,
Hope and resilience, the keys to success impart.
Echoing wisdom sentences, I'd impart,
Amidst market jargon, I'd play my part.

Forward I pressed, with courage and heart,
 Unlocking the essence of triumph, right from the start.
In a business wonderland, where realities did depart,
My unwavering resolve, like encrypted data, my counterpart.

The Triumph's Trail - My Paths to Glory

On the triumph's trail, I'd conquer and chart,

The Triumph's Trail - My Paths to Glory, a journey so smart,

Unlocking achievements, in the corporate cart,

In Wonderland's conquest, where successes restart.

The Courageous Code - My Bravery's Tune

In the courageous code, where valor plays its part,

The Courageous Code - My Bravery's Tune, from the heart,

Unlocking courage, in the corporate's vibrant mart,

In Wonderland's adventures, where courage imparts.

The Resilience Rhapsody - My Strength's Reprise

In the resilience rhapsody, where resilience sparks,

The Resilience Rhapsody - My Strength's Reprise, through the dark,

Unlocking endurance, in the corporate's parks,

In Wonderland's challenges, where resilience marks.

The Encrypted Echo - My Secrets Aloud

In the encrypted echo, where mysteries depart,

The Encrypted Echo - My Secrets Aloud, in the heart,

Unlocking hidden truths, in the corporate art,

In Wonderland's whispers, where secrets impart.

The Digital Dream - My Realities to Chart

In the digital dream, where visions depart,

The Digital Dream - My Realities to Chart, from the heart,

Unlocking the future, in the corporate's chart,

In Wonderland's visions, where dreams restart.

Chapter 113

The Resilient Reawakening

Resilience allows us to bounce back from setbacks

In the corporate enigma, I took a stride,
A cryptic wisdom in the depths did hide.
Resilience, the elixir, by my side,
Bouncing back from setbacks, with it, I'd ride.

Through kaleidoscopic markets, I'd glide,
In Wonderland of commerce, no place to hide.
Resilience, my antidote, deep and wide,
Defeating illusions of defeat, I'd confide.

"Why yield to adversity?" I'd decide,
With resilience, I'd not be denied.
Inner strength, a power, magnified,
In the perplexing dreamscape, I'd take it in stride.

In the labyrinth of mirages, I'd coincide,
Resilience, my magic cloak, my pride.
Catalyst for transformation, a guide,
In this surreal realm, where I'd not be defied.

In cosmic rhythms of markets, I'd bide,
Resilience, recovery's cornerstone, certified.
Echoing wisdom sentences, side by side,
Amidst the enigmatic corridors, I'd be my own guide.

Forward I'd press, my quest personified,

Unlocking the essence of bouncing back, bona fide.

In a realm where the true meaning wouldn't subside,

Amidst business's enigma, I'd rise and ride.

The Bounce-Back Ballad - My Resilience's Dance

In the bounce-back ballad, where setbacks confide,

The Bounce-Back Ballad - My Resilience's Dance, as I stride,

Unlocking my strength, in the corporate tide,

In Wonderland's challenges, where resilience won't hide.

The Visionary Voyage - My Dreams Afloat

In the visionary voyage, where dreams coincide,

The Visionary Voyage - My Dreams Afloat, a vibrant ride,

Unlocking aspirations, in the corporate guide,

In Wonderland's journey, where dreams are allied.

The Dynamic Duet - My Collaborative Flow

In the dynamic duet, where teamwork's certified,

The Dynamic Duet - My Collaborative Flow, side by side,

Unlocking potential, in the corporate wide,

In Wonderland's partnerships, where goals are tied.

The Inspirational Echo - My Wisdom's Lore

In the inspirational echo, where insights provide,

The Inspirational Echo - My Wisdom's Lore, as I decide,

Unlocking knowledge, in the corporate stride,

In Wonderland's wisdom, where truths preside.

Chapter 114

The Dance of Hope and Resilience

Both hope and resilience are essential for overcoming challenges

Amidst corporate mists, surreal lands expand,
A truth profound in this bewildering wonderland.
In the language of business, I take a stand,
Hope and resilience, a cosmic force, hand in hand.

Challenges shifting, like puzzles in the sand,
Hope sparks fires of possibility, unplanned,
Resilience, armor 'gainst adversity's command,
In this corporate realm, I understand.

"Why embrace one alone?" I ask, unplanned,
Hope, North Star, in the darkness grand,
Resilience, an anchor in the tempest's strand,
In this surreal dance, we're bound, as life's band.

In the hallucinatory realm, where dreams expand,
Optimism and determination, success's demand,
Hope and resilience, like yin and yang, stand,
Echoing wisdom sentences, my corporate brand.

Forward I press, in this corporate fairyland,
Hope and resilience, my guiding hand,
Unlocking essence, challenges withstand,
In enigmatic corridors, where my story's planned.

My Hopeful Waltz - Tomorrow's Dance

In the hopeful waltz, where dreams expand,

My Hopeful Waltz - Tomorrow's Dance, hand in hand,

Unlocking tomorrow, in Wonderland's land,

In the corporate symphony, where futures are grand.

My Resilient Rhapsody - Challenges' Refrain

In the resilient rhapsody, where setbacks disband,

My Resilient Rhapsody - Challenges' Refrain, they understand,

Unlocking my strength, in Wonderland's command,

In the corporate journey, where I withstand.

My Visionary Verse - Dreams' Parade

In the visionary verse, where goals are planned,

My Visionary Verse - Dreams' Parade, creatively manned,

Unlocking aspirations, in Wonderland's hand,

In the corporate narrative, where dreams are scanned.

My Inspirational Interlude - Wisdom's Tune

In the inspirational interlude, where insights are in demand,

My Inspirational Interlude - Wisdom's Tune, a knowledge brand,

Unlocking truths, in Wonderland's expanding land,

In the corporate lore, where wisdom's strand.

My Digital Duet - Innovation's Chance

In the digital duet, where tech's advance,

My Digital Duet - Innovation's Chance, they enhance,

Unlocking the future, in Wonderland's trance,

In the corporate cosmos, where innovations entrance.

Chapter 115

The Digital Currency of Love

Love is a fundamental human need

In the virtual labyrinth, where logic and dreams entwine,
My narrator's journey, surreal truths to define,
In corporate visions, a revelation's sign,
Love and connection, in the digital design.

Holographic boardrooms, stock market's incline,
Love not just an emotion, but a fundamental line,
Encoded in my heart, algorithms align,
Compassion's currency, in the code's confine.

"Love, a commodity? In empathy's outline,"
I pondered, thoughts digital, in code's fine,
In the business's hallucination, a truth to divine,
Love's the wellspring, connections entwine.

Transactions and negotiations, a digital storyline,
Connections like fiber optics, a bridge to confide,
Uniting digital dreamers, in a world so benign,
Reality's boundaries, by bonds redefined.

In this surreal domain, where data and emotions combine,
A ballet of algorithms, where sentimentality's the sign,
Love and connection, not mere data on a line,
Wisdom's sentences, in digital interactions, they shine.

Forward I pressed, love's pursuit in my design,

A beacon of guidance, my corporate lifeline,

Unlocking a fulfilling life, my odyssey's outline,

In the corridors of the matrix, love's heartbeat does entwine.

My Loving Overture - Hearts Aflame

In the loving overture, where passions intertwine,

My Loving Overture - Hearts Aflame, a love so fine,

Unlocking emotions, in Wonderland's grand design,

In the corporate story, where hearts combine.

My Compassionate Cadence - Bonds That Grow

In the compassionate cadence, where feelings enshrine,

My Compassionate Cadence - Bonds That Grow, divine,

Unlocking connections, in Wonderland's love line,

In the corporate narrative, where souls align.

My Empathetic Elegy - Kindness' Song

In the empathetic elegy, where empathy does incline,

My Empathetic Elegy - Kindness' Song, a gesture benign,

Unlocking compassion, in Wonderland's embrace, a sign,

In the corporate journey, where deeds define.

My Grateful Gavotte - Thankful Dance

In the grateful gavotte, where gratitude does enshrine,

My Grateful Gavotte - Thankful Dance, hearts entwine,

Unlocking appreciation, in Wonderland's radiant line,

In the corporate symphony, where thanks intertwine.

Chapter 116

The Digital Dance of Connection

Connection with others gives us a sense of belonging and purpose

Amidst the digital labyrinth, my tale of reflection,
In corporate illusions, an unexpected direction,
My quest for meaning, a surreal connection,
In the intricate web, I found life's perfection.

Holographic meetings, virtual handshakes, introspection,
True belonging and purpose, not mere abstraction,
Not algorithms or spreadsheets, but human interaction,
Defined my existence, my life's intersection.

"In networked bonds of collaboration, our soul's correction,"
I mused, thoughts encoded, with digital detection,
In this ethereal landscape, devoid of imperfection,
Threads of connection wove life's profound collection.

Digital interaction, team collaboration, my life's direction,
Connection with others, not a mere affection,
The fuel for my journey, the compass's detection,
In this surreal domain, a revelation's reflection.

Balance between profit and bonds, my deep affection,
The tapestry of reality, a profound connection,
My quest, a dance of algorithms, no defection,
In the intricate web, wisdom's inscription.

Forward I pressed, the pursuit of connection,

A guiding star, my story's reflection,

Unlocking the essence of a life's perfection,

In the corridors of the corporate matrix, my direction.

My Connecting Chorus - Bonds Unbroken

In the connecting chorus, where friendships find protection,

My Connecting Chorus - Bonds Unbroken, a heartfelt collection,

Unlocking loyalty, in Wonderland's connection,

In the corporate symphony, my lifelong affection.

My Collaborative Cadence - Partners in Stride

In the collaborative cadence, where cooperation's our election,

My Collaborative Cadence - Partners in Stride, a shared affection,

Unlocking teamwork, in Wonderland's connection,

In the corporate journey, where goals meet in a cross-section.

My Empathetic Ensemble - Hearts Aligned

In the empathetic ensemble, where compassion's our connection,

My Empathetic Ensemble - Hearts Aligned, in heartfelt reflection,

Unlocking understanding, in Wonderland's affection,

In the corporate narrative, where minds find intersection.

My Grateful Gathering - Thanks Aplenty

In the grateful gathering, where appreciation's our connection,

My Grateful Gathering - Thanks Aplenty, our warm affection,

Unlocking thankfulness, in Wonderland's protection,

In the corporate story, where gratitude's our collection.

Chapter 117

Digital Bonds: Love in the Code

Love and connection help us to thrive and grow as individuals

In the virtual realm of corporate dreams, where data streams,

I found my quest, not confined to dreams,

My longing for love and connection, not what it seems,

For in the digital landscape, it was woven into the schemes.

Lines of code like ethereal threads, in the virtual streams,

Love and connection, not mere whimsical themes,

But algorithms essential, like moonlight's gleams,

For in this surreal place, they held the keys to reams.

As I traversed through meetings, and virtual schemes,

I learned love's not just feelings but much more it deems,

In genuine care for colleagues, clients, and regimes,

My passion for excellence, fueled by love's beams.

Connection, too, in shared goals and virtual regimes,

A sense of unity that broke down physical extremes,

"Is it not in compassion's code and collaboration's streams,"

I pondered, in the language of business, with digital dreams.

In each project's success and data-driven themes,

I saw results of love and connection in extremes,

Strategic assets, not just sentiments in reams,

Fueling my growth, as the wisdom sentence gleams.

In this surreal domain, where business and life seems,

To blend and intertwine, like woven reams,

My quest for love and connection, not just schemes,

But a digital symphony of success, as the wisdom gleams.

I pressed forward, determined, in the corporate schemes,

For love and connection were not just digital dreams,

But transformative elements, as the story beams,

In the digital matrix, where growth and wisdom redeems.

Chapter 118

Love's Kaleidoscope

There are many different ways to experience love and connection

Amid a dreamscape surreal, emotions running wide,
I embarked on a quest, with love as my guide,
In this enchanting realm where affection did reside,
I ventured forth to explore, with heart open wide.

Through clouds of vibrant feelings, like rivers, I did glide,
Each color, a different love, in this landscape, I'd confide,
Romantic, platonic, and more, in every form, I'd ride,
For love's spectrum was diverse, with nothing left to hide.

"Is it not within this tapestry," I mused with heartfelt pride,
"That we find the true essence, in which we're all allied?"
In this dreamscape of emotions, where hearts were side by side,
I saw love's many faces, each with a wisdom to provide.

As I journeyed through this realm, where love's magic did reside,
I learned that love had no bounds, it was vast and open-eyed,
From passionate embraces to friendships bona fide,
Love came in countless forms, with feelings to confide.

In this surreal dreamscape, where emotions took their flight,
I celebrated love's diverse, enchanting light,
Each connection was a gem, each bond shining bright,
In the kaleidoscope of love, I found my heart's delight.

My quest for love and connection, an odyssey untied,

A journey into human bonds, where souls felt unified,

For every variation of love, like stars in the night sky,

Held its own wisdom sentence, in life's grand lullaby.

With love as my compass, I'd journey far and wide,

In the surreal narrative of affection, I'd abide,

Unlocking the essence of diverse love, I'd take it in stride,

In a dreamscape where the heart's true story could never be denied.

My Love-Filled Canvas - Hearts' Artistry

In the love-filled canvas, where emotions coincide,

My Love-Filled Canvas - Hearts' Artistry, where love won't subside,

Unlocking the spectrum, where love does reside,

In the corporate portrait, where hearts' artistry is my guide.

My Affectionate Ballroom - Emotions' Dance

In the affectionate ballroom, where feelings do confide,

My Affectionate Ballroom - Emotions' Dance, side by side,

Unlocking sentiments, on this heartfelt ride,

In the corporate gala, where emotions' dance is my pride.

My Compassionate Cadence - Kindness Unveiled

In the compassionate cadence, where goodwill does provide,

My Compassionate Cadence - Kindness Unveiled, a benevolent stride,

Unlocking generosity, with hearts open wide,

In the corporate ode, where kindness does reside.

My Grateful Waltz - Thanks and Cheers

In the grateful waltz, where appreciation does reside,

My Grateful Waltz - Thanks and Cheers, heartfelt and bona fide,

Unlocking thankfulness, on this gratitude ride,

In the corporate ballad, where thanks and cheers coincide.

My Unified Ballet - Hearts in Unison

In the unified ballet, where unity's the guide,

My Unified Ballet - Hearts in Unison, a feeling magnified,

Unlocking oneness, with love as my pride,

In the corporate story, where hearts in unison confide.

Chapter 119

Love's Luminous Tapestry

We can find love in our relationships with family, friends, partners, and pets

In the realm of emotions, surreal and vast,
I embarked on a journey to unearth, at last,
The intricate web of bonds, the ties that hold so fast,
Love's constellation patterns in the heart's starry cast.

Deeper into the dreamscape, I would venture on,
To find that love's embrace was never truly gone,
Not just in romance's glow, where hearts were drawn,
But in friendships' laughter and family bonds at dawn.

"Is it not in the bonds we weave," I pondered then,
"That love's radiant tapestry is stitched with golden pen?"
In the surreal realm of heart, the truth did brightly ken,
Love's facets multifaceted, like a precious gem.

In the surreal whirlwind of my feelings, I did find,
That love was an endless well, a balm for the soul's bind,
In the laughter shared with friends, in family intertwined,
Even in my pet's antics, love's warmth did I remind.

Love flowed free and boundless, an eternal stream,
Nurturing the soul's garden, like a cherished dream,
Each connection held a lesson, a wisdom to redeem,
A profound truth of love, like a star's radiant gleam.

In the dreamscape of emotions, where the heart did roam,
I celebrated bonds and connections, making love my home,
Each relationship, a facet of love's precious tome,
In every moment's embrace, I felt love's sweet poem.

With each discovery, my heart did take flight,
In the tapestry of emotions, I found love's pure light,
A wisdom sentence, like a star in the darkest night,
"Love's essence is everywhere, in all, it's shining bright."

And so, I journeyed on, with love's flame aglow,
In love's luminous tapestry, I found my flow,
A celebration of connections, in joy and woe,
In the surreal dreamscape of emotions, love's grand tableau.

Chapter 120

Love's Unveiled Tapestry

We can also find love in our communities, through our work, and through our hobbies and interests

In life's grand tapestry, I did embark,
To find love's gentle whisper in the most unlikely arc,
Beyond romantic notions, where love could disembark,
In every corner of existence, I'd seek its spark.

Within the warm embrace of my community's kin,
Neighbors bound by love, like family from within,
In the bonds of camaraderie, I saw love's hidden grin,
A love unspoken, yet strong, beneath the neighborly din.

At work, colleagues became companions on the way,
Shared passions forged connections, like the light of day,
A different kind of romance, in the tasks we'd convey,
Love's embrace in teamwork, where hearts would sway.

Hobbies and interests, where enthusiasm would ignite,
In shared pursuits, love's sparks would shine so bright,
Camaraderie abounding, like stars in the velvet night,
Love in every laughter, in every shared delight.

"In the tapestry of life," I mused, "love does firmly dwell,
Woven in each thread, in every tale we tell,
Not confined by boundaries, not trapped in a single cell,
In countless forms it thrives, a story to retell."

In the tapestry of existence, love did truly bloom,

Not limited by tradition, nor confined to any room,

It flourished in diversity, dispelling any gloom,

A boundless, endless love, like nature's sweet perfume.

So I journeyed on, my heart forever wise,

In love's diverse expressions, I found my prize,

A wisdom sentence bloomed, like stars in endless skies,

"Love's essence everywhere, in every moment, it lies."

With this newfound wisdom, I embraced love's art,

In every form it took, in every beating heart,

In life's grand tapestry, I played my part,

Discovering love's magic, a treasure to impart.

Chapter 121

The Weaver of Change

Change is a natural part of life

In life's grand tapestry, where destinies entwine,
Change, the thread eternal, in every life, a sign,
Not to be feared, but embraced, as a friend divine,
I learned, in this tale of mine.

I gazed upon seasons, a dance of sun and rain,
Winter's icy grip, yielding to spring's gentle strain,
Technology's evolution, an ever-growing chain,
Change, the common theme, in joy and in pain.

"Change," I declared, "is progress's grand old sage,
A sculptor of life, on wisdom's very stage,
Just like the caterpillar, in its transient cage,
Change brings forth beauty, as we turn the page."

A wisdom sentence bloomed, a beacon in my hand,
"Embrace change's embrace, across sea and land,
For in its tender care, life's mysteries we'll understand,
In transformation's arms, our destinies are planned."

With this newfound wisdom, I journeyed on,
In the company of change, my fears were gone,
With each new dawn, a brand-new song,
In the embrace of transformation, I truly belonged.

So I pressed ahead, through life's shifting range,

Knowing change was the weaver, of stories to exchange,

In its intricate pattern, there was nothing strange,

Just the endless potential, of growth and renewal's change.

My Ever-Adapting Tango - Dance of Evolution

In the ever-adapting tango, where change takes stage,

My Ever-Adapting Tango - Dance of Evolution, a wisdom-filled page,

Unlocking transformations, as life's endless engage,

In the corporate theater, where change scripts its wage.

My Resilient Symphony - Notes of Endurance

In the resilient symphony, where challenges I'd engage,

My Resilient Symphony - Notes of Endurance, a resilient cage,

Unlocking strength, like a bird uncaged,

In the corporate opera, where resilience writes its message.

My Creative Waltz - Imagination's Flight

In the creative waltz, where dreams I'd engage,

My Creative Waltz - Imagination's Flight, on creativity's stage,

Unlocking ideas, like a boundless sage,

In the corporate gallery, where creativity paints its image.

My Infinite Overture - Possibilities Aplenty

In the infinite overture, where opportunities I'd engage,

My Infinite Overture - Possibilities Aplenty, on life's expansive stage,

Unlocking potential, like a wisdom sage,

In the corporate arena, where possibilities script their page.

Chapter 122

The Crucible of Change

Transformation can be a positive and empowering experience

In life's ever-turning pages, I found,

A truth profound, in transformations unbound,

Like phoenixes rising, from ashes on the ground,

Change, my ally, in its power I was crowned.

I saw resilience bloom, amidst trials and test,

People emerging stronger, at their very best,

In life's crucible, I put doubt to rest,

Change, my companion, on this ardent quest.

"Change," I declared, "is the crucible of our might,

Where we forge our strength, like steel in the night,

Through trials we rise, with courage and insight,

With each transformation, we reach a wondrous height."

A wisdom sentence formed, a treasure to uphold,

"Embrace transformation, let its story be told,

In its embrace, our destiny we'll unfold,

With empowerment and positivity, our spirits will be bold."

With newfound belief, I journeyed on,

In the heart of transformation,

I'd be drawn, Empowerment my shield, in the early dawn,

With positivity, life's symphony was reborn.

So I pressed on, through the changes I'd face,

In the crucible of life, I'd find my place,

With empowerment and positivity's grace,

In transformation's embrace, a wondrous chase.

In the end, I discovered, through every turn and range,

That change was a catalyst, its power so strange,

In life's crucible, I'd embrace the change,

And emerge empowered, a heart set to arrange.

My Change Symphony - A Dynamic Movement

In the change symphony, where life's movements I arrange,

My Change Symphony - A Dynamic Movement, a beautiful exchange,

Unlocking transitions, with the winds of change,

In the grand theater of existence, where destinies interchange.

My Evolving Waltz - Dance of Renewal

In the evolving waltz, where growth I arrange,

My Evolving Waltz - Dance of Renewal, a continuous exchange,

Unlocking rebirth, as seasons rearrange,

In the cosmic ballroom, where cycles estrange.

My Resilient Opera - Acts of Transformation

In the resilient opera, where courage I arrange,

My Resilient Opera - Acts of Transformation, a courageous exchange,

Unlocking metamorphosis, as life's stages rearrange,

In the grand narrative of existence, where stories derange.

My Creative Ballet - Artistry's Flourish

In the creative ballet, where innovation I arrange,

My Creative Ballet - Artistry's Flourish, a creative exchange,

Unlocking masterpieces, as inspiration I'd arrange,

In the vibrant gallery, where expressions arrange.

My Harmonious Symphony - Unity's Permanence

In the harmonious symphony, where hearts I arrange,

My Harmonious Symphony - Unity's Permanence,

a harmonious exchange, Unlocking bonds, as souls I'd arrange,

In the grand concerto of existence, where connections rearrange.

Chapter 123

The Bridge to a Brighter Tomorrow

Change and transformation can lead to a better life

In life's grand tapestry, with twists and with spins,
I discovered, through thick and through thins,
A truth simple yet deep, as the universe grins,
Change and transformation lead to where joy begins.

I watched as those open to change's gentle call,
Found happiness and contentment, standing tall,
In life's ever-shifting, miraculous thrall,
Adapting and growing, they enthralled.

"Change," I proclaimed, "is life's wondrous bridge,
To a future more brilliant, no need to hedge,
Transformation's the key, let's rid of the cage,
In its chrysalis, a butterfly takes center stage."

My wisdom sentence, a gem to convey,
"Change and transformation, our guides on the way,
To a better existence, in the light of the day,
With each twist and turn, let joy come what may."

With newfound insight, my spirit did soar,
Through each change and transformation I'd explore,
A better life beckoned, at the heart's very core,
In this wondrous journey, forevermore.

So I journeyed ahead, through the day and the night,

In the realm of transformation, I took my flight,

Building bridges to joy, in the soft, golden light,

With change as my ally, everything felt just right.

In the end, I discovered, through life's twists and its churns,

That change was a teacher, from which the heart learns,

With transformation as guide, in each twist it discerns,

A bridge to a brighter tomorrow, where happiness returns.

My Wisdom Waltz - Lessons of Change

In the wisdom waltz, where insights I'd earn,

My Wisdom Waltz - Lessons of Change, an illuminating churn,

Unlocking knowledge, in every twist's discern,

In the grand library of existence, where wisdom's pages turn.

My Resilient Rhapsody - Melody of Growth

In the resilient rhapsody, where strength I'd discern,

My Resilient Rhapsody - Melody of Growth, a powerful churn,

Unlocking resilience, in every twist's discern,

In the orchestration of existence, where courage's flames burn.

My Creative Canvas - Painting Life's Turns

In the creative canvas, where artistry I'd discern,

My Creative Canvas - Painting Life's Turns, a creative churn,

Unlocking masterpieces, in every twist's discern,

In the gallery of existence, where expressions yearn.

Chapter 124

The Dance of Openness

We can embrace change and transformation by being open to new experiences

In a world where change did endlessly roam,
A truth in my heart did foam,
That to embrace transformation and find a new home,
I must stay open, wherever I'd roam.

For those who'd adventure with open arms wide,
Found change was a friend, with nothing to hide,
They'd grow and transform on this magical ride,
In the ebb and flow of life's changing tide.

"Openness," I declared, "is the key, don't you see?
To embrace every change, to let life's river be free,
New experiences shape us, like leaves on a tree,
In the ever-evolving script, we're the authors to be."

With this newfound wisdom, like a guiding star bright,
I journeyed ahead, through day and through night,
Embracing each change, with my heart taking flight,
Open to life's dance, in the soft, golden light.

My wisdom sentence profound, a truth to convey,
"Openness to newness, let it guide your own way,
In change and in transformation, let it hold sway,
As you dance with life's rhythm, come what may."

In the end, I discovered, in the tale I unfurled,

That openness was a gift, a gem in life's pearl,

With each change and transformation, I'd twirl, In the graceful,

endless dance of this wonderful world.

My Openness Overture - Embracing the Unfamiliar

In the openness overture, where new horizons I'd twirl,

My Openness Overture - Embracing the Unfamiliar, an adventure
unfurl,

Unlocking experiences, as life's colorful banners swirl,

In the vast tapestry of existence, where curiosity would whirl.

My Insightful Interlude - Illumination's Gaze

In the insightful interlude, where wisdom's light I'd twirl,

My Insightful Interlude - Illumination's Gaze, a knowledge whirl,

Unlocking enlightenment, as truths within me curl,

In the infinite library of existence, where wisdom's lanterns twirl.

My Courageous Cadence - Facing the Abyss

In the courageous cadence, where fears I'd confront and twirl,

My Courageous Cadence - Facing the Abyss, a bravery whirl,

Unlocking bravery, as inner demons I'd hurl,

In the labyrinth of existence, where courage's banners unfurl.

My Transformational Tune - Evolution's Song

In the transformational tune, where changes I'd embrace and twirl,

My Transformational Tune - Evolution's Song, a life's journey swirl,

Unlocking evolution, as old selves I'd unfurl,

In the grand theater of existence, where growth's banners whirl.

Chapter 125

The Scholar of Life

We can learn from our experiences and grow from them

In a tale of old, where wisdom did gleam,
I lived as one who held life as a flowing stream,
A scholar of lessons, in day and in dream,
With eyes wide open, I'd always esteem.

To me, life was school, every day a new page,
In the grand book of learning, I'd often engage,
Challenges and triumphs, in every life stage,
Held treasures of wisdom, like a wise sage.

When troubles did beckon, I'd ponder and say,
"What can I glean from this trying day?
A lesson, a blessing, in life's grand display,
Shall guide my path, come what may."

And in moments of joy, when success did bestow,
I'd celebrate, let my happiness flow,
Reflecting on lessons, I'd come to know,
"How can this wisdom, in me, further grow?"

My secret to growth, both simple and grand,
Embrace every moment, in life's tender hand,
With heart and with mind, I'd always understand,
That every experience was wisdom's own brand.

My wisdom sentence, a truth to bestow,

"Every experience, let it be high or low,

Is a chance to learn, to flourish and grow,

In the grand school of life, let your wisdom flow."

In the end, I found, as the years gently rolled,

The journey of learning was more precious than gold,

A life filled with wisdom, a story well-told,

In the boundless adventure of growing, I'd hold.

My Reflective Rhapsody - Wisdom's Echo

In the reflective rhapsody, where life's tales I'd behold,

My Reflective Rhapsody - Wisdom's Echo, in stories untold,

Unlocking insights, as memories in my heart unfold,

In the timeless library of existence, where wisdom's stories enfold.

My Timeless Tango - Moments in Harmony

In the timeless tango, where memories I'd gently hold,

My Timeless Tango - Moments in Harmony, in memories' gold,

Unlocking nostalgia, as cherished moments are retold,

In the cherished album of existence, where heartstrings are consoled.

My Soulful Sonata - Life's Melodic Verse

In the soulful sonata, where experiences are treasured and told,

My Soulful Sonata - Life's Melodic Verse, in journeys bold,

Unlocking melodies, as life's songs gracefully unfold,

In the grand symphony of existence, where destinies are foretold.

My Grateful Gavotte - Heartfelt Acknowledgment

In the grateful gavotte, where gratitude I'd enfold,

My Grateful Gavotte - Heartfelt Acknowledgment, in appreciation's mold,

Unlocking thankfulness, as blessings in my heart hold,

In the cherished moments of existence, where gratitude's stories are told.

My Everlasting Epilogue - A Life Well Lived

In the everlasting epilogue, where legacies I'd extol,

My Everlasting Epilogue - A Life Well Lived, in memories that console,

Unlocking the essence of a life's gentle toll,

In the grand tapestry of existence, where souls find their eternal role.